Able Children
in
Ordinary Schools

Deborah Eyre

David Fulton Publishers
2 Park Square, Milton Park, Abingdon, Oxon OX14 4RN

270 Madison Avenue, New York, NY 10016

First published in Great Britain by David Fulton Publishers 1997
Transferred to digital printing

David Fulton Publishers is an imprint of the Taylor & Francis Group, an informa business

Copyright © Deborah Eyre 1997

British Library Cataloguing in Publication Data

A catalogue record for this book is available from the British Library.

ISBN 1-85346-441-4

Typeset by The Harrington Consultancy Ltd, London

Contents

Acknowledgements

I am grateful to many people who have helped to shape my understanding of the issues surrounding the education of able children and who have patiently responded to my endless questions and requests for information. In particular I am grateful to Tom Marjoram and to Johanna Raffan who have supported my work for many years.

I should like to thank all those in NACE for their ideas and encouragement and the many individual schools and LEA officers who have shared their thinking and documentation with me, in particular Michael Turner, Kevin Lambert, Joan Freeman, Fil Came, Roy Kennard, Catherine Clark, Sue Mordecai, Sue Leyden, Scott Hurd, Chris Webster, Peter Tilsley, Frankie Williams, Peter Williams, Frankie Gaywood, Yvonne Perret, Chris Stevens and Donna Vernon.

Oxfordshire LEA has been the experimental base for my work on able children and I would like to thank them for their support. Individuals within the LEA have contributed greatly to my work, and I would like to thank Penny Hollander, Geoff Dean, Jean Clark, Giti Paulin, Rebecca Ungpakorn, the Early Years Team, Rob Reynolds and Geoff Jones. Especial thanks to Lucy Oliver for her day-to-day encouragement and to Richard Howard with whom I have shared many useful educational discussions. Thanks too to all the Oxfordshire teachers and schools with whom I work, and in particular those represented in the Secondary Schools network; Susan Blake and Susan Macmillan for writing material for this book, and Matthew Arnold School, Marston Middle School and Frideswide Middle School for sharing their documentation.

Thanks to Westminster College, Barry Carpenter and David Fulton Publishers; the award to me of the 1996/97 Fulton Fellowship led to my writing this book. Finally, thanks to my family who have all contributed in some way: my husband John for proof-reading and other advice, my son Richard for his computer skills, and my daughter Judith for her unfailing encouragement and support.

Deborah Eyre
September 1996

Preface

The purpose of this book is to help teachers of able children in ordinary schools. Very little has been written in Britain about the education of able children, although there is a wide body of research in other parts of the world. What has been written has been primarily from the psychologist's viewpoint or has focused on individual or groups of able children. Such research as has been carried out into provision has focused on selected groups of able children operating in optimum conditions. Both of these elements provide useful information for the teacher but neither is, in itself, sufficient to enable ordinary schools to plan effective provision for their able pupils. A system of school-based provision must not only take account of what is desirable for able children but also what is possible within the constraints of an ordinary school.

Some may ask whether an ordinary school is the appropriate location for the education of able pupils. This is not an easy question to answer. Selective schools have some advantages for the most able: pace is likely to be rapid, there is the chance to work with others of like ability and expectation is high. However, the grammar school system was dismantled because it was deemed to be unfair and unsuccessful for the country as a whole. Pupils in the lower streams of the grammar schools failed to thrive, the 11+ was unreliable as an indicator of eventual performance, and children who were not accepted into grammar school saw themselves labelled as failures at age 11.

Recent research into ability indicates that it is impossible to predict with any certainty which children will eventually be the high achievers. Not only is innate ability needed but also opportunity, support, motivation and hard work. This leads to some politically sensitive conclusions in respect of selection. A selective school could, in itself, provide the opportunity, but how could schools take into account support, hard work and motivation when making their selections?

In many ways these arguments are academic. Most parents are happy with their comprehensive schools and geography dictates that choice of school is only an issue for those who live in urban conurbations or who have transport to take their child elsewhere. Most children, including the most able, are at present educated in mixed ability primary schools and then in comprehensive schools. The Assisted Places Scheme, which allows able pupils to be taught in selective schools, only caters for 1 per cent of the school population, which is a very small percentage of the able pupils in school.

Therefore, in considering educational provision for able children, there is a clear need to focus on provision in ordinary schools. The 1988 and 1993 Education Acts have set the framework for education in state schools and it is within that context that discussions regarding provision for the most able should take place. In addition, the needs of able pupils cannot be separated from broader educational initiatives such as the move to raise standards, league tables for secondary schools, the underachievement of boys, the debates into the teaching of basic skills, etc.

It is certainly timely for a focus on provision for able children in state schools as their needs have largely been ignored since the demise of the grammar school system. Able children have been seen as a low priority for many schools and have received very little attention from individual teachers. Guidance for schools from the School's Curriculum and Assessment Authority (SCAA) has been non-existent and from the Department for Education and Employment (DfEE) minimal.

However, there has been a quiet revolution taking place in some parts of the teaching profession regarding this issue, and the approaches which have been developed are highly respected at international level. This was recognized by the DfEE in 1993 in the form of a small grant to NACE (National Association for Able Children in Education) to develop this work and share good practice. At the heart of this work is the recognition that the number of pupils who have significant ability is much greater than had previously been considered. This is because previous assessment methods had always relied on the identification of all-round or overall ability. This is fairly rare, but significant ability in certain subjects is more plentiful: outstanding musicians may not be good at history, good mathematicians may not be good at art, etc. A focus on specific ability as well as all-round ability helps to maximize pupil potential and has the added advantage of helping to raise school standards and examination results.

The existence of so many children with subject-specific abilities, coupled with the uncertainties of selection procedures, leads to a strong case for the education of able children to take place in comprehensive schools offering appropriate provision. The education of able pupils in ordinary schools should not, therefore, be seen as making the best of a poor system but in fact as the optimum provision. Many American school districts which used to have Gifted Children programmes have now decided that better provision can be made within the context of the ordinary school.

Of course the key point to recognize is that good education for able children in ordinary schools does not happen by chance: it takes careful planning, development work and monitoring. It is difficult to achieve and needs the involvement of a wide variety of staff. But it is possible. In some LEAs, including my own (Oxfordshire), a limited amount of training and support is available to assist schools in developing their provision for able children. Our experience in Oxfordshire shows that it can take a number of years for a school to become more effective in its provision for able children, and there is a need for extensive staff development if anything useful is to be achieved. This book aims to assist schools in their quest for better provision for able children in ordinary schools. It draws on research into the characteristics of able children and effective provision, and it sets them within the context of the 1988 and 1993 Education Acts and the National Curriculum. It shows practical ways to extend pupils based on a sound theoretical basis.

By helping able children to maximize their potential in ordinary schools we should enable them to lead fulfilled lives and to make a significant contribution to society.

Chapter 1

Defining Able Children

The education of able pupils in maintained (state) schools since the introduction of comprehensive schools has often been described as the 'Cinderella' of education provision. Some educationalists have included able pupils in the category of newly disadvantaged groups. Reasons for this include the lack of legislation concerning the needs and rights of able pupils, the lack of government guidance on effective provision for able pupils at a time when guidance in other areas is extensive, and the lack of nominated funding for staff training or school-based development work. This view emerges from research findings of a range of educational sources. A typical sample is:

> In the case of the most able groups the work was considerably less well-matched than for average and less able groups. (HMI, 1978, p.81)
> High attainers were underestimated on 40% of tasks assigned to them. (Bennett *et al.*, 1984, p.215)
> In the majority of schools the expectations of very able pupils are not sufficiently high. (HMI, 1992, p.28)

However, at the same time as these points are being made by some sectors of the educational establishment, others assert that the whole of the British education system is geared towards meeting the needs of a small percentage of academically able youngsters at the expense of the vast majority of the population. The latter group, in making their case, point to the use of the academically-based GCSE, and the A Level 'gold standard' in most school sixth forms. The Dearing 16–19 Review (DfEE, 1996) recognized this academic focus in highlighting the need for a broader range of educational qualifications to reward a wider range of achievements. How then can two such radically differing viewpoints co-exist?

Perhaps the GCSE, which is such a barrier for many pupils, is not in fact sufficiently challenging for the most able. Perhaps the mere existence of such a standard leads schools to focus on gaining A to C grades at GCSE rather than on maximizing the potential of individual pupils. Certainly this whole preoccupation with GCSE does little to affect provision for able pupils in the primary school or even in the early years of the secondary school. Rather than seeing the education system as tilted in favour of the academically able it would be more sensible to view the GCSE issue as a problem related to the existence of an arbitrary measure, of an arbitrary range of subjects and skills, at an arbitrary time in a pupil's education.

The purposes of this chapter are: to explore the factors that have led to such educational confusion; to consider some of the major issues facing schools as they attempt to define 'able pupils'; to consider the nature of ability – what we mean by an able child and whether there is educational agreement on this definition; and to explore the link between ability and achievement – are these two terms, often used interchangeably by teachers, the same thing? Unless these issues are carefully considered it is impossible for a school to develop a coherent approach to the nurturing of ability.

Researchers such as Francis Galton (1822–1911) were confident that intelligence was singular, was carried in the head and could be reliably measured by psychometric testing. These ideas of a genetically-inherited superior mind became the basis of the traditionalist view of intelligence. Terman (1925) in the first, and still largest, longitudinal study of gifted children, used psychometric testing as the basis of his selection procedure. During the twentieth century the traditionalist viewpoint has largely been replaced by a wider view of intelligence. Creativity in particular is not measured as part of an intelligence test, but since the work of Guilford (1950) it has come to be recognized by many as an aspect of intelligence. More recently ideas have emerged which suggest that intelligence should be seen as constituting a series of 'intelligences' covering a range of components. There are many advocates for this pluralist approach but perhaps the best known to most teachers is Gardner (1983).

IQ as a measure of intelligence

In my experience most people, both teachers and the general public, still hold the view of a single general intelligence (IQ) which children have to a greater or lesser extent and which can be accurately measured on an intelligence test; hence the request from many primary school teachers and parents for an intelligence test to confirm the ability of a child. Frequently teachers say that they think they have an able child in their class but would like an intelligence test administered to confirm their hypothesis.

The fact that such a view remains dominant, at least in England and Wales, is perhaps to some extent a legacy of the 1944 Education Act. This act was rooted firmly in the view that intelligence was inherent and measurable, and that those with different levels of intelligence needed different types of education. Grammar schools, secondary modern schools and technical schools were established to meet the needs of children with different levels of intelligence. The reasons for the dismantling of this system and the introduction of comprehensive schools were, at least in part, a recognition of the system's failure. There were without doubt some issues related to inequality of funding between types of schools, but a major educational reason was the inaccuracy of the 11+ examination. Famous examples exist of pupils rejected as unsuitable for grammar school who went on to gain doctorates at university or become highly successful in their chosen sphere. Either the 11+ had failed to measure intelligence accurately or an intelligence quotient could change as a child developed.

Many teachers recognize these historical flaws but see them as related to borderline grammar school entrants, not to problems with the selection of able pupils. They continue to believe that it is possible to define a child's level of ability by the use of a test and to give it a numerical score. Perhaps this is because traditionally the causes of learning deficits have been identified through the use of tests, or perhaps it is simply part of an unrealistic search for an ideal way to categorize children.

Individual teachers are, however, not alone in their continuing faith in the IQ system. Some psychologists still believe that it is possible to measure intelligence through psychometric testing and they continue to seek more accurate measures, e.g. Jensen (1980), Eysenck (1981) and Bouchard *et al.* (1990). The American Gifted Children programmes in many states relied on psychometric testing for selection until well into the 1980s and some still use them. In England, MENSA has remained a high-profile advocate of intelligence testing and a new association, Children of High Intelligence (CHI) has been formed for children with high IQs. The National Association for Gifted Children (NAGC), a parental pressure group, until very recently advocated better provision for gifted children in schools, based on a single intelligence platform.

However, the main body of research into intelligence indicates that the link between high IQ and high achievement is under review. Freeman (1995, p.15) states:

> The assumption that a high IQ is essential for outstanding achievement is giving way to recognition of the vital role of support and example, knowledge acquisition, and personal attributes such as motivation, self-discipline, curiosity, and a drive for autonomy – all this being present at the right developmental time.

A multi-dimensional view of ability

The vast majority of psychologists in the second half of the twentieth century see ability as being made up of a number of factors. In the first place, traditional ideas of ability being linked only to cognitive domains and their development in school have given way to a focus on a broader range of abilities (music, art, sport) and to a consideration of lifelong learning and achievement. Even within the cognitive range it is now accepted that elements in addition to IQ, such as creativity, are important. Also, the achievements of a child in school are not always reflected in later performance. For some children conditions at school or in their home life may mean that they do not fulfil their potential during conventional schooling. Equally, these may lead to lower or accelerated performance at certain times in the child's school career.

Ability in art, sport or music has come to be recognized as comparable with cognitive ability and in equal need of nurturing. If a school is looking to identify those with cognitive abilities they should also consider those with ability in music, art and sport.

In defining a multi-dimensional view of giftedness, simple ideas have given way to increasingly complex ones. Creativity, since the work of Guilford (1950), has been seen by many psychologists as an essential aspect of giftedness. It is the component which differentiates between those who do well and those who do brilliantly. Sternberg (1985),

4

Cropley (1995) and Urban (1990) are all leading figures in this field. Psychologists with an interest in creativity have tried both to define it and to measure it. Urban's model of creativity (Figure 1.1) illustrates well the complexity in this single component.

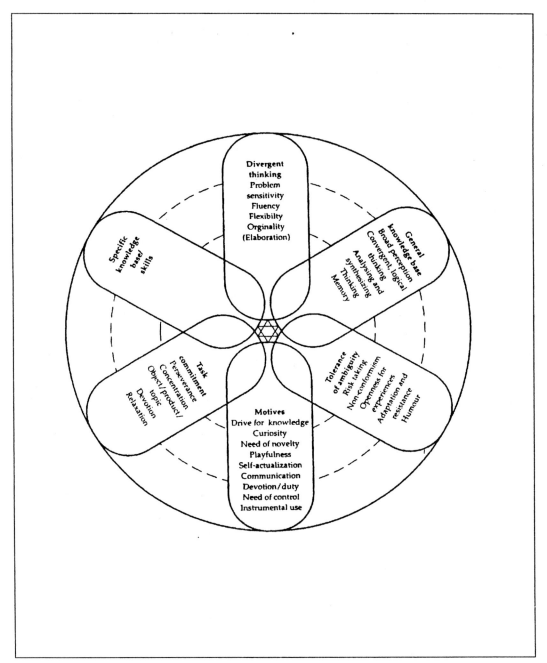

Figure 1.1 Urban's component model of creativity

Renzulli (1977) defined giftedness more widely by suggesting that it included not only ability and creativity but also task commitment (Figure 1.2).

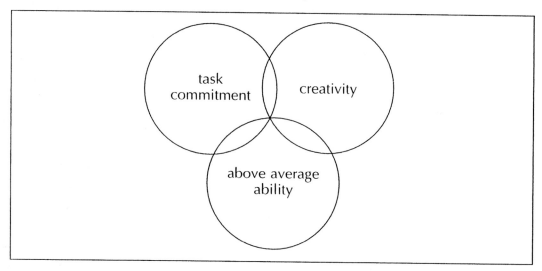

Figure 1.2 Renzulli rings

Sternberg (1985) put forward his 'triarchic theory' which included componential, experimental and contextual elements. Mönks (1992, see Figure 1.3), Gagné (1994, see Figure 1.4) and others have added the influence of home, school and peers – the element of opportunity and support which seems to be so influential in converting potential into achievement.

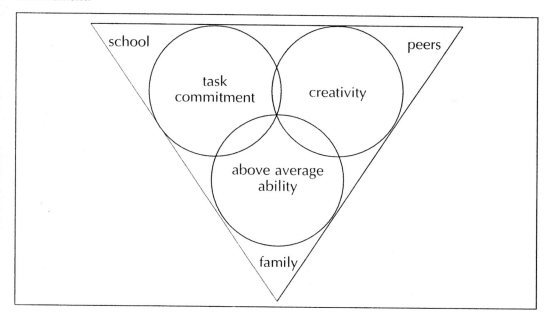

Figure 1.3 A multifactional model of giftedness (Mönks, 1992)

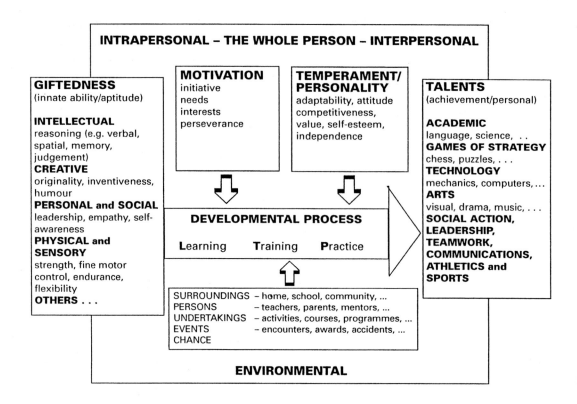

Figure 1.4 Gagné's modified model for the more able and exceptionally able

Finally, one should mention the work of Gardner (1983), with his focus on multiple intelligences: 'Genius is likely to be specific to particular contexts: human beings have evolved to exhibit several intelligences and not draw variously on one flexible intelligence'. Gardner recognizes seven relatively autonomous forms of ability (see Figure 1.5, Krechevsky and Gardner, 1990). A child may be able in any one or any combination of these: just because a child excels in one area it is not obvious that he or she will excel in others.

❖ LINGUISTIC OR VERBAL
❖ SPATIAL – MOTOR
❖ LOGICAL – MATHEMATICAL (numerical)
❖ MUSICAL
❖ BODILY – KINAESTHETIC (physical)
❖ INTERPERSONAL (social)
❖ INTRAPERSONAL (self-knowledge)

Figure 1.5 Multiple intelligences

For those of us whose interest in this area lies in the implications for schools, the array of research may at first be daunting. No wonder a simple test of IQ seems more appealing to some. However, the really important implication for schools is simple: ability is complex, it is made up of a range of factors, some of which it is impossible to measure effectively. If a school uses a broad definition of ability (encompassing not only ability in academic subjects but also in art, music and sport) and it recognizes the role of creativity, motivation and opportunity, then its methods for the identification and nurturing of such ability will be complex.

The link between ability and achievement

In recent years there have been several retrospective studies looking at the early lives of people who went on to become high achievers. Bloom (1985) considered the top 200 Americans in a range of specialisms, from mathematics to swimming, music to brain surgery. Howe (1995) looked at the early lives of geniuses. Evidence from these kinds of studies began to indicate that many high achievers did not show outstanding ability or precocious talent in early life. Therefore the search for a test of reliable indicators of ability in early childhood may prove of limited value in terms of determining future success.

These findings are of immense significance for teachers and educators. They mean that a child's performance at age 5, as judged against the mean, may be very different from a child's performance at 11 or 14. Schools consistently expect children to develop at an even pace and, although teachers are aware of the possibility of late development, etc., the organizational systems rarely take account of this. The top group or set often remains the same and the most able pupils who are identified at entry to secondary school in Year 7 often remain the most able cohort throughout their time at the school.

From the point of view of the individual child this is an interesting area. There are without doubt significant numbers of children who do not show outstanding talent in the early years but who go on to achieve highly at GCSE and A Level. They may not be among the best mathematicians in the class, but may later go on to outstrip them in terms of performance. They may be slow to develop the secretarial skills of writing and punctuation but later develop a style of great maturity. Equally, there are children who at age 5 appear to be exceptional in their ability but who seem to plateau out by the end of the primary school. Observing this across a whole LEA, I at first attributed this decline in performance to the teaching and opportunities in Key Stage 2 (7–11 years). Further investigation suggests a different and more complex conclusion linked to motivation, opportunities and parental influence.

What makes success

There seem to be three separate components which together lead to outstanding educational achievement:

- innate ability,
- opportunity/support,
- motivation/hard work.

Interestingly it does not seem necessary to have an equal distribution of all three. Children who have ability and a great deal of motivation, but little opportunity and very little support, sometimes succeed against the odds. Children with strong family support and good opportunities achieve without outstanding ability or motivation. Children with ability, support and opportunity sometimes fail to achieve through lack of personal motivation.

Innate ability

This is a child's natural aptitudes and skills. Whilst it may not be possible to measure ability accurately, it is possible to observe its existence and to measure it approximately. Observing young children it is obvious that some have advanced ability in particular areas. Some children for example never make grammatical mistakes: no one has taught them grammatical structure but they seem to have a natural facility with language which enables them to work with it in a complex way. Others have a facility with numbers: they understand conservation of number very early and have no difficulty in working with large numbers or in recognizing patterns within number. Others have an ability to connect information, making sense of their world by linking new experiences to their existing ideas. These types of characteristics are early indicators of ability.

As a child moves through school these natural aptitudes often allow for rapid development and advanced performance. The child who has always had a feel for language is likely to enjoy English and be a high achiever throughout school. Mathematical children retain their fascination with number and achieve highly. However, sometimes children stop showing their initial flair. Discouraging comments from teachers, peer comments and lack of family appreciation can all lead to this potential not being developed.

Opportunity/support

This is part of the nature/nurture debate. A supportive environment with appropriate opportunities can be highly influential in terms of achievement. Perhaps this is why so many middle-class children are identified as 'able'. Opportunity is the key to success. A talented young violinist does not need a maestro to teach him or her the violin from an early age, but they do need a violin teacher and a violin. Children need books, resources, equipment and encouragement if they are to achieve highly.

During the late 1960s selection was largely rejected by British educationalists, and mixed ability teaching became the norm. Opportunities for able pupils diminished in many schools. Pupils who were achieving at an acceptable level were given little attention or encouragement to achieve more highly. A general belief existed that able pupils would always be successful regardless of their circumstances. HMI (1992, p.28) stated: 'In the majority of schools the expectations for very able pupils are not sufficiently high. The provision for these pupils is patchy and is often not seen as a priority'.

However, research indicates that support and encouragement are vital to success. Freeman (1991), in her fascinating account of gifted children growing up, points conclusively to the influence of both school and family in supporting able children. Where such support was not available, promise was often not fulfilled. Perhaps her harshest criticisms are reserved for comprehensive schools. Even those pupils who went to comprehensive schools and were successful appear to have achieved in spite of their schooling. 'Many believed that they could have done a lot better academically at a selective school.' (Freeman, 1991, p.129).

My own experiences of the comprehensive system are more optimistic. Comprehensive schools can provide their most able pupils with good opportunities, and my work with Oxfordshire schools has shown me numerous examples of comprehensive schools providing both a general strategy for their most able pupils and encouragement for individuals. However, there is no room for complacency: many able children in comprehensive schools (including Oxfordshire schools) do not have appropriate encouragement and support and massive under-achievement is the result.

Motivation/hard work

Genius is 99% perspiration and1% inspiration. (Thomas Edison)

Recent research points increasingly to the role of personal motivation and hard work in achieving success. Although it may sometimes appear that able children make great leaps in their learning without having to work hard, they are in fact working towards that leap. Howe (1995, p.37) describes it thus:

> Exceptional people climb higher than the rest of us do, though they may also climb faster and more efficiently. But they do climb all the same, just like everyone else. No one miraculously arrives at the peak of their accomplishments.

This is a very important factor for schools in their work on able pupils, because it highlights the need for an ethos or climate of hard work if high achievement is to be the result. The all-too prevalent climate in many English schools, where it is 'not cool to be bright', is highly damaging to pupil achievement. Able pupils will not strive to achieve unless such achievement is suitably recognized and rewarded.

For individual children the message is clear: innate ability and good opportunities are not enough to ensure success. The child must want to achieve and must strive to achieve highly. As children move through school this element becomes more and more significant. Rudduck (1995) cites Years 10 and 11 as a period when many pupils realize that they should have established good work patterns earlier. This trend is just as significant for able children as for others: able pupils may have found it possible to coast through school doing the minimum of work, but they are unlikely then to excel in GCSE. However, the strong role of motivation and hard work also enables some pupils of above average, but not outstanding, ability to achieve highly, especially if the opportunities and support are good.

The lessons for schools

1. Intelligence is more than a singular inherited IQ.
2. It is impossible to test intelligence by the use of a single psychometric test and so identification must include qualitative data.
3. Intelligence is made up of a series of components and is multi-dimensional.
4. A child's ability is influenced by opportunities, support and motivation, and therefore the performance of able children may vary as they move through school.
5. Opportunities and support are vital to success and children need access to them in both home and school.

6. Schools have a significant impact on the achievements of able children and any idea that the school does not need to pay attention to such pupils will lead to extensive under-achievement.

7. Comprehensive schools can provide for able pupils but many choose to give them low priority and so inhibit their achievements.

8. Able children need to work hard if they are to succeed. A school needs a culture that encourages hard work and which recognizes and rewards achievement.

9. Motivation is a significant factor in success. Above average pupils with strong personal motivation are likely to be as successful as pupils with outstanding ability but less motivation.

10. Using a wide definition of ability, the numbers of children who might be described as 'able' in some areas are significant and therefore all schools have some able pupils.

Chapter 2

Identification

Background

The purpose of this chapter is to assist schools in establishing appropriate school-based identification systems. The most important prerequisite of such systems is that they should fit neatly with the existing structures and systems so that the identification of ability and talent can be an integral part of the school's activities. Experience with Oxfordshire schools would indicate that it is only in schools where the identification is embedded in school-based systems that it has significant impact on classroom practice. Otherwise, the link between identification and provision is tenuous: although certain pupils may have been identified, this process has not led to a change in classroom provision for those children. This chapter demonstrates how the identification of able pupils can be built into existing school systems and suggests methods for implementation, coordination and monitoring.

In recent years the NACE/DfEE project (Supporting the Education of Able Pupils in Maintained Schools), and others, have established models for the identification of able pupils in schools. Many LEAs publish guidelines for their schools based on this work. This chapter looks beyond initial implementation and highlights some of the more complex issues which have emerged when schools have adopted this kind of approach and used it over a number of years. It also explores in some detail the range of possible identification methods and discusses their individual strengths and limitations. For schools establishing identification systems for the first time, this chapter should help to ensure an effective approach as well as highlighting some of the possible pitfalls and difficulties. For schools which already identify their most able, this chapter suggests ways to make the process more rigorous. Partial or inaccurate identification may in fact be more harmful than no identification, since pupils may be actively excluded rather than passively ignored.

It is vitally important that state schools identify their most able pupils. The idea that able pupils will always do well and do not need particular attention is discredited. Lack of effective, planned provision leads to disenchantment and under-achievement. It leads to an education system in which pupils will only succeed if they have not only ability but also the desire to conform and do well, since they will gain little support and encouragement from teachers. It also leads to an unfair system of provision-on-demand. Those children whose parents alert the school to their child's ability and press for suitable provision may have their needs met. Other less fortunate children will not. If schools are not systematic and proactive in recognizing ability and providing appropriate support, then pupils from disadvantaged backgrounds will be penalized and the children of white middle-class parents withdrawn from the state sector. Recognizing able pupils is not an optional extra; it is an essential aspect of providing for good, comprehensive education.

Research implications

As ideas on the definition of ability have changed over the years so too have methods of identification. A long period of reliance on the value of intelligence and other psychometric tests has given way to an understanding of the need to use both quantitative and qualitative methods. Howe (1995, p.35) states:

> The moral is clear: if you want to know which children are likely to succeed, don't put all your eggs in the IQ basket. It is very unlikely that we will ever discover a test that can be administered in childhood that will reliably predict eventual adult outcome.

Most teachers are aware of the limitations of intelligence testing and indeed many can remember personally the problems associated with the 11+. A leader in *The Guardian* of the time (14 February 1966) included the following comments:

> For schoolchildren at least, intelligence testing is now beyond the pale. The 11-plus, by almost common consent was unfair, inefficient and sometimes vicious in its effects. Even in areas opposed to comprehensive change, like Bournemouth, it is being decently buried.

It is however interesting that at the same time as psychologists are recognizing the complexity of ability and the interaction between ability and opportunity, school systems are moving back towards a reliance on quantitative data. This is not entirely surprising, in that the school agenda has, in the past 15 years, been driven by a political imperative as well as an educational one. Qualitative information such as teacher assessment has been viewed politically as 'soft' and unreliable, and quantitative data such as tests and league tables as indisputably more rigorous. This has been part of the undermining of teachers as professionals, whose opinions are seen as politically left-wing and woolly. *This kind of agenda has had a significant impact on the identification of able children. Teachers already tentative in identifying the most able have resorted to a greater reliance on tests.*

It is not the intention of this book to report in detail on the body of research into ability – this is already well documented by others – but rather to consider the implications of research findings for school decision-makers. Whilst central government is encouraging a greater reliance on testing, educational researchers are suggesting that testing is of limited value in recognizing high ability. Montgomery (1996, p.27) states:

Researchers now ask what kinds of ability constitutes giftedness, how these abilities are organized and how they interact. Traditional tests of cognitive abilities are being used to define patterns rather than levels, and there is an increasing interest in and emphasis upon cognitive structures and processes. The analysis and development of metacognitive abilities, problem solving and non-cognitive aspects, such as motivation, values and attitudes, self image, confidence and dedication, social abilities and values, are some of the more recent and most important areas of investigation and development in identification of the able. All of these new developments put identification more in the hands of teachers than before.

Clearly this is significant. Teachers are recognized as having a major role to play in the identification of able children but at the same time they are less confident in making assessments than ever before. All those setting education policy, including SCAA and LEAs, will need to provide guidance and training for teachers if they are to play a greater role in the identification of able children. Equally heads and senior managers will need to lead their staff and support them in developing appropriate skills. Identification is at best a difficult and inexact science. Teachers cannot be expected to be effective in identifying able pupils unless they are given appropriate training and support.

Identification in the secondary school

Many of the issues related to the identification of able pupils are not phase-specific; they are equally relevant at Key Stage 1 or at Key Stage 4. The major differences lie in the types of systems which are likely to be employed. In the primary school, systems will rely heavily on the professional opinion of one class teacher, supplemented by a range of other quantitative and qualitative data. Here there is an in-depth knowledge of the individual child but potential for problems related to recognizing subject-specific abilities. In the secondary school, subject ability recognition should be less of a problem, but having pupils taught by a range of teachers can lead to a lack of appreciation of a child's overall ability or performance. Hence the maths teacher may be unaware that his outstanding mathematician has difficulty with history and geography, and the humanities staff may be unaware of the child's mathematical ability. Most secondary staff assume that pupils perform in other subjects in the same way as they perform in theirs, largely because they have no information to the contrary. Identification in the secondary school is not only about 'talent spotting' but also sharing information. This enables the school to build up a picture of those with specific abilities, those whose abilities come in clusters of related subjects and those who have all-round ability.

Purpose

The identification of able pupils is not an end in itself. There is only value in identifying ability if it leads to better provision in subject departments and a better match of work to individuals. If departments are to differentiate to meet a range of ability then teachers will need some indication of those for whom the more challenging work will be appropriate. Identification is also helpful in the selection of pupils for setting, for enrichment or enhancement activities and for monitoring purposes. It is however my experience that some schools become so immersed in the process and procedures of identification that its purpose becomes obscured. Individual teachers provide information on pupils but do not see this as affecting their own teaching. Identification has become an end in itself. The school has detailed lists and data on the performance of individuals but these impact not at all on provision for pupils in the classroom.

Perhaps some of the difficulty here emanates from the desire to create a clearly defined cohort. This can only be done effectively if the cohort is restricted to those with all-round ability otherwise the numbers become too great. Some schools which include able pupils within their special needs departments also attempt to use the Code of Practice (DfEE, 1994) methodology as the basis of their work on able pupils. In my opinion, these techniques, which focus on individual programmes of work, are only suited to truly exceptional pupils. They are simply too burdensome for wider usage. A subject teacher cannot be expected to provide individual work for large numbers of pupils or the classwork will lose clarity and it becomes impossible to track progress. A small number of pupils (a nominal 2 per cent) may benefit from individualized provision and additional monitoring. These pupils will need more than class-based differentiation. They may need to work with older pupils or take exams early. They are truly pupils with special educational needs.

Identification of the most able is at best imprecise. Its main purpose should be to ensure that teachers are in a good position to match work to the pupils in their class, i.e. in any lesson the teacher should know who, in general terms, could benefit from extension. In an ideal world, each teacher would know the abilities of each individual in the class in detail. In the secondary context this is impossible, especially in curriculum areas where teaching is less frequent. If you teach a class once a fortnight, then it takes a long time to appreciate individual needs.

However, even imprecise identification can provide a good starting point for teachers. If it is recognized as such, then the information on the able pupils list becomes a kind of hypothesis. The individual teacher uses it as the basis for planning but adjusts future planning to take account of the pupils' responses. In this way the teacher either begins to confirm the hypothesis or to gather evidence for a different view. Eventually some pupils will be found who consistently need extension but were not identified on the original list, and whose names will be added for future teachers. Equally there may be one or two pupils for whom the original assessment has proved to be over-optimistic. These warrant further investigation. Are they underachieving? Was the original assessment inaccurate? This list *should* become more rigorous as the pupils move through the school and as each teacher's experience of those pupils is taken into account.

Another useful purpose is as part of the monitoring of individuals. If a pupil is identified as having high ability in a subject or subjects, then their assessment, progress tests, etc., should reflect this. If a dip in performance occurs, then it can easily be spotted by the form tutor and action taken accordingly. In the same way, pupils identified as more able in a subject or subjects should have appropriate work targets. As part of target-setting procedures, the form tutor can use the able pupil list as an *aide-mémoire* when reviewing whether the targets set are appropriate.

This type of approach to identification is clearly quite different from the traditional view. The able pupil list or register is a working document which is continually subject to change and adjustment. Inclusion on or exclusion from the list becomes less important if it is seen as less definitive.

One difficulty which often exists in schools when considering able pupils is the fear that any method of identification of ability is a form of selection. Of course in a way it is, but if we are ever to be effective in matching work to pupil need then certain types of selection are inherent in the process. For a comprehensive school to provide effectively for its most able, some setting and streaming is essential but selection on entry is not.

The purpose of identification of able pupils in the secondary school is to improve provision by creating a more informed picture of pupils' abilities and talents. No school-based identification system is likely to be perfect, but striving to make it as comprehensive as possible will assist both teacher planning and pupil monitoring.

Confidentiality

Some schools have attempted to identify their most able pupils using a variety of methods and have subsequently created a register or list containing this information. In the model described in the section above, such information would be used to inform the planning of all teachers, and would therefore need to be made available to all teachers. There may be some rationale for suggesting that each subject department needs only details of its own subject area in order to create provision. However, I would suggest that a key element in the identification procedures is the opportunity to gain a picture of the whole child, across all subjects. As a subject teacher it is easy to assume that pupils perform in other subjects in the same way as they perform in yours; if they are amongst the most able in your subject then this will be replicated in other subjects, and if they are average in your subject they will be average in others. Evidence indicates otherwise, and knowing that a child performs differently in other subjects may cause teachers to look more carefully at the individual.

It is the practice in some schools for able pupil data to be made available only to selected staff. This may be the able pupil coordinator plus the senior management team, or may include heads of department. The reasons given for restricted access are mostly concerned with test scores but also, in some instances, with teacher nomination. These lists are seen as sensitive material which could be misused. Whilst appreciating the possible sensitivities involved, I find this approach difficult to uphold. My own view is that teachers should be trusted to deal with sensitive information appropriately. However, if that is not deemed possible, then the data must be translated into a coded form which can be circulated to all staff. *Teachers must know who has been identified if the identification is to have impact on teaching and learning. Otherwise the whole process is pointless.*

This issue gives a fascinating insight into the way in which our society views ability and achievement. If pupils are scoring highly and doing well, then they should have that achievement recognized. If we, as schools, have to hide evidence of high achievement in a locked filing cabinet, then the message we send to pupils is confused. No wonder pupils say, 'It's not cool to be bright'.

Identification methods in the secondary school

The key factor in effective identification is the use of as many sources of information as possible. Some of the evidence may be contradictory, for example tests scores may not confirm the view of a teacher or parents, or parents and teachers may disagree. Therefore a strategy that recognizes such possible conflicts must be developed. The availability of spreadsheets and databases has made the logging of information in secondary schools much easier, and it is now possible to see at a glance a child's performance in a wide range of areas.

In establishing an identification procedure, the school needs to clarify the occasions within the school cycle when data will be added or reviewed, and also when the information, in total or in distilled versions, will be conveyed to staff.

Methods of identification are numerous but some of those most commonly used in secondary schools are as follows:

1. Information from primary schools.

2. Tests, both summative (SATs, NFER, etc.) and progress tests and exams.

3. Teacher nomination, based on subject-specific checklists and departmental criteria.

4. Classroom observation.

5. Peer and self-nomination.

6. Parental nomination.

All of these methods have strengths but also limitations. All staff need to be familiar with the advantages and the problems if the methods are to be useful.

1. Information from primary schools

In theory, schooling should be a seamless process with information passing from school to school as the child progresses. In practice, the transfer of information is fraught with difficulties: what to transfer, how to use it, whether there is consistency across schools. These are not solely issues for able pupils, but they have a great significance for able pupils since poor transfer documentation often leads to their 'marking time' in Year 7.

Many secondary schools have worked with their primary schools both on issues related to the transfer of information and on issues of curriculum continuity. The National Curriculum has provided an agenda for discussion prior to secondary transfer. The National Curriculum levels assume that pupils will enter secondary school having reached, on average, Level 4. Able pupils will be reaching Levels 5 or 6. Whilst teachers recognize this in theory, in practice levels ascribed to individual pupils are often the subject of disagreement between schools.

Teacher assessment is difficult since no system for moderation across schools exists. Many secondary schools which work closely with their partner primaries evolve their own systems for interpreting information from schools. A Level 5 from school A would be assessed at Level 4 in school B, etc. Where best practice exists, schools have established regular opportunities for moderation discussions and this has enhanced greatly the continuity between schools. All schools in this type of partnership have a working understanding of what constitutes achievement at Level 5/6, perhaps through a portfolio of examples of children's work.

The biggest practical barrier to such work has been the introduction of greater parental choice. At a conference in London, a colleague from Norfolk explained how his school worked with five feeder schools to develop effective curriculum continuity. The model was excellent but will not transfer. In Oxfordshire a secondary school typically takes from about

20 primary schools. A London head explained at the same conference that his school took from 64 schools in the previous year; making effective professional links with so many schools is an impossible task.

Even where the information flow is good, the information may not be in a form that can be used easily. Many primary schools send a file on each child to the secondary school, but the information in this cannot be conveyed effectively to all the teachers who teach that child in Year 7. Therefore, either the information is only read by the year tutor, or it is used as an instrument to create mixed ability groups or sets. Many teachers in fact start teaching Year 7 groups with little information on the general ability level or standard reached by those children when in primary school. *If 'marking time' is to be avoided, then each teacher must have basic information on pupils of high ability in the same way as they do special needs information.*

As with many aspects of able pupil provision, there is no simple answer to this dilemma. For rural schools or for town schools with a limited number of feeder primaries, the work on curriculum continuity between subject teachers in the secondary school and colleagues in primary schools may be the best route forward. The development of greater professional trust should ensure that Year 7 teachers feel confident in using the primary school assessment as the basis for their medium- and short-term planning. Extensive partnership work does assist assessment, as well as having many other advantages.

For schools with a more diverse intake, a different approach may be needed. The secondary school could take a lead in requesting information on able pupils using a subject-based approach, and also for outstanding leadership or other qualities. This lacks the rigour of moderated assessment but is at least a starting point. Experience indicates that primary teachers are generally quite reluctant to identify children as 'more able' in transfer records, largely because of the difficulty of knowing how such pupils will perform in the bigger secondary cohort. Research by Nebesnuick (1993) shows a significant discrepancy between the assessment of able pupils by their primary teachers and subsequently by Year 7 teachers. Reasons for this are explored more fully in the section on primary school identification, later in this chapter.

Information from primary schools is therefore an important aspect of the identification of able children in the secondary school. It is the first source of information that teachers receive about the pupils in Year 7 and should provide the basis for future work. All teachers of Year 7 need to know if a child has been identified, either by SATs or teacher assessment, as being of high ability in their subjects. It should be recognized that, for all the reasons outlined above, some of these assessments may prove to be inaccurate, but Year 7 teachers must use them as a starting point rather than wasting time until they are able to make their own assessments.

From the senior management perspective, there is a broader issue to consider: how can the data from primary schools on able pupils be made more reliable? What can the secondary school do to facilitate this? A systematic focus on this area of work has considerable advantages for a school:

- it increases pupil and parent satisfaction;
- smooth continuity ensures that 'marking time' is avoided and therefore pupil progress will be more rapid;

- standards achieved should be higher;
- teachers will look more closely at individuals if they know they will be required to nominate their most able.

All these aspects help to raise standards for a wide range of pupils including those identified as more able in a subject or subjects, hence HMI states (1992, p.viii):

> Where specific attention was given to the needs of very able children there was often a general increase in the level of expectation of all pupils and this was sometimes reflected in improved public examination results.

2. Tests

Tests are used by secondary schools at a variety of points in a pupil's educational experience. They are used to fulfil many functions ranging from the diagnostic to the summative.

Tests used as part of the identification of able pupils can be either individual or blanket tests. There is certainly no shortage of tests available in either category, and the problem for schools is generally which tests to use and when. As far as testing of individual pupils is concerned, this tends to be largely the domain of the Special Educational Needs Department. They, or sometimes an educational psychologist, can test for specific abilities in certain areas or for general abilities. Montgomery (1996) lists the current range of tests available and provides a useful assessment of their advantages and limitations.

Blanket tests are often used in Year 7 to give some indication of the abilities of pupils entering the school. Of course, if primary-secondary continuity were really effective, these would become unnecessary, but at the present time they provide a pragmatic solution to the problem of providing baseline information. Such information has increased significantly in recent years as the focus on A–C grades at GCSE has been challenged by the idea of value-added education. In order to assess a value-added element, it is of course necessary to identify a starting point. From the perspective of those interested in teaching and learning, this baseline also gives an opportunity to improve differentiation and target-setting. Therefore many schools now use blanket tests in Year 7 to provide information on the abilities of pupils. NFER produces a range of tests that schools may use, the most comprehensive at present being the Cognitive Abilities Test (CAT). This test is undertaken in three sections and provides data on verbal, non-verbal and quantitative abilities. Some schools have experienced difficulties with this test. It is, by its nature, quite an intimidating test and may not prove particularly inviting to Year 7 students new to the school. This is especially so for less able pupils, but may also influence timid or under-confident pupils. It takes three sessions to administer and must be marked and analysed. Because of these problems of time, cost and suitability, some schools have used simpler tests – only the non-verbal element, or a verbal reasoning test. If only one test element is to be used, then the non-verbal may produce the most helpful information, as many of the school's other reading, spelling and progress tests will be verbally-oriented.

Blanket test information may be held by senior management to develop value-added data but should also be used by teachers to enable better matching of work to pupils' abilities. In the identification of able pupils, those who score highly on any element of the test should be added to the able pupil register. Other tests, including Year 9 SATs, will provide additional information, and those scoring highly should also be included on the able pupil list. In this way the database of information on able pupils will continue to grow.

SATs should not be given greater credence than other forms of identification, as they have all the arbitrary nature of any summative test. Some pupils perform well in exam conditions, others do not. Some able pupils make errors because they cannot conceive that the answer could be so simple. Some refuse to complete the test because it is routine and dull. High performance is also directly related to the amount of work covered by the school, and so able pupils in schools with low expectations may not have covered the higher level concepts. In addition, the SATs simply examine an element of the subject in question and only in the three core subjects of maths, science and English. Therefore, high achievers in other areas may be overlooked. At best one could say that SATs help to identify some able pupils, but certainly not all.

3. Teacher nomination

A significant and powerful form of identification is that of the teacher. Teachers can become highly effective in recognizing signs of ability in their classrooms. One strength of this approach to identification is that, once a teacher recognizes ability, she or he tends to provide for it. Identification and provision have always been seen as closely linked, in that good provision allows ability to be displayed, whilst good identification leads to provision. Figure 2.1 (from Tilsley 1995, Figure 2) describes this idea neatly.

Over the past decade, Oxfordshire LEA schools and some schools within the NACE/DfEE Project have worked to develop their teacher-based identification skills through the use of criteria checklists. This process usually starts with departmental meetings in which each department creates a checklist of characteristics of ability in its subject. This first stage often involves heated departmental debate and raises a range of issues surrounding ability and achievement. Is the ability to write up experiments a characteristic of scientific ability? Can you recognize a good modern linguistic in Year 7? etc.

The process is all-important here, in that in order to help pupils to progress to the highest levels within a subject we must be clear about what it is we want to nurture and develop. This is particularly significant if one takes the Vygotskian view of learning, which links high levels of performance to the support of the teacher (Vygotsky, 1978).

It is always tempting in education to use someone else's ideas to avoid excessive overwork. Some good subject-based checklists do exist; see Figure 2.2 (from Kennard, 1996, p.53), for example. As regards departmental criteria, it may be helpful to use examples for discussion, but a simple incorporation of someone else's approach into the departmental handbook will not be effective. It is the thinking, the reflecting and the consideration of the implications for teaching which are crucial to the success of the exercise.

Having created the checklist, this is then used in the second or third term of Year 7 to nominate pupils of high ability in each subject area. This is usually done using a grid (like the one shown in Figure 2.3) and the results fed directly into the computer from each department to allow for comparison with other data.

It is worth saying something here about Oxfordshire schools' findings over the last five years. First, identification in some subjects is more accurate than in others. This is consistent with research by Denton and Postlethwaite (1985). Teachers who teach a subject frequently to the same class are better able to recognize their most able pupils. Therefore core subjects

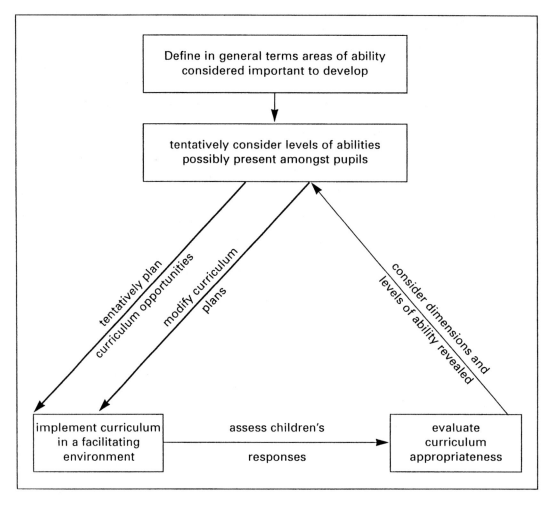

Figure 2.1 Tilsley's model for identification

– English, maths and science – fare better than other subjects. This is a significant finding not only for Year 7 but also for short courses in Years 10 and 11. Dave Smith of Chipping Norton School investigated this link as part of his work for the Oxfordshire Achievement Project (Oxfordshire LEA, 1988) and found that, where teachers taught classes as part of a 'modular circus', they were less able to assess pupil capabilities effectively.

A second finding from Oxfordshire concerns the difficulties in recognizing ability in French in Year 7. French departments in all schools nominated a greater proportion of pupils as being able than other departments. This may be linked to pupils' enthusiasm for a new subject or to an inability to recognize aptitude at this stage.

Another significant finding concerns the implementation of this kind of approach over a number of years. Denton and Postlethwaite only considered a 'one-off' approach to identification. Work in Oxfordshire schools shows that, over the years, teachers using teacher nomination as part of their cycle of identification become increasingly accurate. This may be linked to knowing from the start of the year that such data will be required in terms 2 and

Structure of mathematical abilities
Able children have the ability to:
Grasp the formal structure of a problem in a way that leads to ideas for action.
Generalise from the study of examples. *Search for and recognise pattern, specialise and conjecture.* Generalise approaches to problem solving.
Reason in a logical way and as a consequence develop chains of reasoning. *Verifying, justifying, proving.*
Use mathematical symbols as part of the thinking process.
Think flexibly; adapt their ways of approaching problems and switch from one mode of thought to another.
Reverse their direction of thought. Work forwards and backwards in an attempt to solve a problem.
Leave out intermediate steps in a logical argument and think in abbreviated mathematical forms.
Remember generalised mathematical relationships, problem types, generalised ways of approaching problems and patterns of reasoning.

Figure 2.2 Kennard's structure of mathematical abilities

Nomination Grid   MARKED APTITUDES

Surname	Class	Tests			Mths	Eng	Sci	Hum	Art	PE	Mus	IT	

Figure 2.3 A grid for recording marked aptitude

3. Therefore, throughout the year, prior to the actual nomination, the teacher is developing a mental list based on evidence of performance in class. This allows plenty of time to experiment – to ask an individual particularly searching questions or to offer an especially challenging task. The advantage of this is that the teacher nomination exercise becomes the culmination of the identification process rather than the start of it. Hence pupils are not waiting until terms 2 or 3 to receive extension opportunities. Teacher nomination should be reviewed on an annual basis in Years 7, 8 and 9.

An effective way to use teacher data is in juxtaposition with blanket test data. This provides a useful tool for identifying possible under-achievement and also helps to focus on individuals. Teachers need to be encouraged not to view any discrepancy found here as indicating that either their judgement or the tests' findings are 'wrong', rather that these discrepancies may illuminate more complex aspects of ability of an individual pupil. A meeting of heads of department may discuss any unusual findings and initiate appropriate action. See Figure 2.4 for a worked example.

4. Classroom observation

The ability of some able pupils is easily identified. Highly articulate students or those who produce written work of a consistently high standard are usually recognized in class. However, large classes and busy teachers mean that it is possible to overlook the quieter, more conforming child or the hesitant child with little belief in his or her own capabilities. If we see part of the school's role as 'talent spotting', then exploring ways to uncover covert ability is important.

The opportunity to use another adult in the classroom to observe is often rare in school, but when available it is highly effective. Possible avenues here include the use of students and non-teaching staff as well as colleagues. Also, 'talent spotting' can be combined with other activities, for example inter-class visiting as part of the development of departmental continuity, or LEA monitoring.

5. Peer and self-nomination

Involving pupils in their learning has become a major focus for many schools in recent years. Records of achievement, target setting and personal profiles have all encouraged pupils to reflect upon their own capabilities and performance. This has certainly made a useful contribution to the identification of able pupils. Discussions between individual pupils and their teachers have helped some pupils recognize their potential as well as worked to eliminate areas of difficulty.

Peer recognition and nomination is less well developed in British schools. Research indicates (Crocker, 1988) that even young children are able to recognize ability in others and can also rank themselves academically. Certainly discussions with students in secondary school would indicate a clear consensus on the strengths and weaknesses of particular individuals. Yet the school system does little to involve pupils in recognizing and rewarding achievement. Perhaps if they were more actively involved, then achievement would be more highly valued in the secondary school.

Work has been done in both the USA and Canada on the usefulness of peer recognition.

LEARNING SUPPORT DEPARTMENT

Subject identification of More Able Pupils in Year 8, March 1992.

There are 206 pupils in Year 8. In total, 102 (49.5%) pupils were nominated by subject teachers. Apart from any other conclusions we can draw, this is a staggering number and indicates the potential our pupils have, ranging from abilities in one subject to those who are achieving across the curriculum in as many as nine subjects.

I have tabulated the NVRQ (Non-Verbal Reasoning Quotient) scores next to the results of the survey. This standardised test is a good indicator of reasoning and thinking skills. The average score is 115 and any number over 125 is a good score; any number over 134 is excellent!

BREAKDOWN OF DATA

42 (20.4%) pupils received single subject nominations. All departments are represented in this category except Modern Languages (CDT and ART have still to be submitted). The largest single subject nominations were in PE/Games. Peter Jones stands out with a high NVRQ score (132). 10 pupils have scores over 120.

26 (12.6%) of pupils were targeted in 2 subjects. Four of these pupils have NVRQ scores over 120 which indicates that they could be underachieving. Particularly Ian Smith who had a very high score of 132.

As the nominations increased, the numbers of children declined in each category, as we would expect.

11 (5.3%) pupils were named by 3 subject teachers. Again, 4 pupils had good NVRQ scores, notably Raymond Jones (130).

7 (3.4%) students received 4 nominations. Their NVRQ scores are good indicators of performance in this category. Both Anne Smith and Richard Gordon have very high NVRQ scores of over 135.

5 (2.4%) in the 5 subject bracket. Solid NVRQ scores reinforce their nominations.

8 (3.9%) pupils fall into the 6 subject category. Michael Watts and Rachel Butterworth have lower than average NVRQ results.

The top 2% have equivalent NVRQ scores, please note Daniel Watson of 8R who received 7 nominations (NVRQ 138).

The zero nomination category needs particular note. We have here 8 pupils with high NVRQ scores: Clare Taylor and Graham Reynolds have scored 134. Although this constitutes only 3.9% of the whole year group and could pay tribute to the accuracy of our subjective methods of identification, these pupils represent 22% of those with NVRQ score of over 121.

The Learning Support Department will continue to monitor the pupils on the list. As a department we can offer support for these pupils in cross curricular activities, such as the residential courses on Astronomy, Geology and Archaeology which have been successful in the past. Departments can bid for our time, either to free (by covering the classes) the subject specialist to take out a group of able pupils for enrichment or extension work or to prepare resources. We can recommend, on occasions supply and sometimes deliver enrichment resources.

Thank you for your cooperation in compiling this information.

Sue Macmillan.

Figure 2.4 Departmental summary from The Henry Box School

In Britain, some work on this has been undertaken as part of 'circle time' in primary schools and occasionally as part of PSE in secondary schools, but the British culture does not facilitate such work. Praise between peers is not a significant feature of adult life and many feel uncomfortable when praise is too fulsome.

As peers are effective in the identification of ability, a school may consider it worth exploring ways to harness such information.

6. Parental nomination

'Parental nomination' always brings a smile to the lips of teachers when mentioned in in-service work. All teachers can recall the occasional parents whose perception of their child's ability is wholly unrealistic or whose demands have been so excessive as to cause anxiety in both school and child. In reality such instances are rare, and a school's system should not be based on such exceptions.

Some schools ask parents of prospective pupils whether they think their child has any particular abilities or talents, as part of their induction documentation. Most parents are conservative in their estimations of their children's abilities but are grateful for the opportunity to express their views. Those pupils who are nominated by their parents as falling into the more able category or having specific abilities are added to the able pupil register. Occasionally the parents' view is not shared by the school, but this is openly discussed at parents' evenings.

Summary

Effective identification procedures are usually extensive and permeate all aspects of the school structure. They are not a 'bolt-on' activity. Mapping the available data and feeding them in a useful form to individual departments and staff is often more of a problem for good schools than is the collection of the data.

Statistically, around 40 per cent of the cohort of an average comprehensive school are likely to have been identified as able in something or other (where 'able' means being in the top 10 per cent of the cohort for that subject/aspect). This makes the monitoring of individual provision unwieldy and beyond the scope of the able pupil coordinator. Coordinators are most effective where they gather and disseminate data, deal with issues related to particular individuals, and remind departments of their responsibilities to provide and monitor.

The 40 per cent statistic is also a cause for celebration and one reason why the neat, tidy approach to selection is unhelpful. A cursory look at identification of able children may lead one to assume that it is possible to select a top 10 or 5 per cent or whatever. In-depth evidence suggests that such an approach would exclude large numbers of pupils who have significant ability in a limited range of domains. A good comprehensive school should be able to provide for the whole 40 per cent by offering extension in all subjects and matching it to the pupils who could benefit.

Identification in the primary school

For many primary teachers the process of identifying able children as a whole-school activity may at first appear pointless. Surely teachers know which of their class might be described as more able? This of course presupposes a clear agreement on the nature of ability and the evidence of such ability. In practice neither of these exists in most primary schools and there is much confusion regarding this whole area of work.

Research into the identification of able pupils on transfer from primary to secondary school (Nebesnuick, 1993) shows that the types of phrases used by primary teachers to describe able pupils tend to be linked to ways of working rather than cognitive ability. Here are some examples:

School A	School B	School C
good reader	good reader	good reader
well motivated	neat worker	accurate worker
able to work independently	accurate worker	uses his/her initiative
able to mix easily with adults	mature and extensive vocabulary	can work independently
	well motivated	
	able to work independently	
	enjoys adult company	

These types of comments demonstrate a certain awareness of the existence of able children but also a confusion about the characteristics of ability.

Another piece of research (Burgess, 1996) shows a school with a different issue. In this case children who had been identified as able mathematicians in Year 2 showed varying performance on Key Stage 1 SATs. Further investigation highlighted the way in which the Key Stage 1 SATs assessed only numerically-based aspects of maths and failed to reward children whose abilities fell within other mathematical areas. This school's system for the identification of mathematicians was more thorough than the SATs tests since it was based on a broader range of mathematical criteria.

These two examples illustrate certain points along the identification continuum, the school in Burgess' work being far more rigorous in its identification procedures than the Nebesnuick schools. Although this is often thought to be the case, schools do not, in reality, become adept at identifying able children and then move straight into effective provision. Schools become more effective in identifying able children as they get better at providing for them.

Stages on the identification continuum

Schools generally move through five stages before they become effective in their identification procedures. Some schools move through the five stages quickly, others seem to become stuck in a particular stage and will need a concerted push to move them on to better identification. Stages on the identification continuum are:

1. Awareness of need and value of identification.

2. Ad hoc identification.

3. Test-based identification.

4. School-based systems.

5. A professional approach.

1. Awareness of need and value of identification

At this stage the school is beginning to recognize the need to identify able children. A teacher may have attended a course or conference and fed back to staff the advantages of identification and the problems of possible under-achievement which may result from non-identification. Alternatively, the school may have had an INSET day on this subject or the issue may have been raised for other reasons. Inspection is often the catalyst for encouraging a school to consider able children. Often at this stage, a school knows what it should be doing and why, but has very little understanding of how.

2. Ad hoc identification

For most schools the move from stage 1 to stage 2 is rapid. Once a school realizes that it should identify its most able children, it is likely to make attempts to do so. Staff may be asked to identify the able children in their class, the school may add able children to their special needs documentation and may even create a register of able children. Governors and parents may be informed and the recommended insertion be made in the school prospectus. At this stage some schools consider they have dealt with the issue. In reality, this is the stage where there is most likely to be a gap between policy and practice. The special needs policy records the philosophical approach and the identification system ensures that children who need special provision are identified.

What this stage does not recognize is the level of understanding which individual teachers may have regarding the characteristics of ability. In Oxfordshire schools (Eyre, 1994), the vast majority of primary schools (85 per cent) included able children in their special needs policy. An examination of the entries, however, would indicate a lack of real understanding of the issues involved, and rather more of a formulaic response.

Therefore the types of comments recorded in Nebesnuick's research (1993) would be typical. Teachers, when pressed to give reasons for their identification of individuals, would make very general statements. In School C of Nebesnuick's research, there were two Year 6 classes. The criteria used for selecting able children were different in each class. In all three schools the children identified were hard working and well motivated and had parents who were actively involved with the school. This type of ill-informed identification can lead to bias and inaccuracy. The preoccupation with neat, tidy, conforming children is reflected in informal work undertaken by OFSTED, which indicates a higher than expected number of white middle-class children being identified in inner city schools. The identification was not so much about whether children exhibited the cognitive characteristics associated with able children but more about whether they exhibited the characteristics valued by the teacher and the school.

Even the one curriculum-based comment – 'good reader' – is ambiguous. 'Good reader' could mean able to decode any text no matter how complex; it could mean avid reader who reads extensively for pleasure, or it could mean able to look for different layers of meaning within the text. Only the latter would be an indicator of high linguistic ability.

Therefore at stage 2 of the process, identification is likely to be inaccurate and probably biased, well-meaning but ineffective, and unlikely to influence classroom provision. It could even be dangerous, leading to some children with real potential being overlooked.

3. Test-based identification

This stage sometimes results from a build-up of frustration resulting from stage 2 (the 'someone give me an answer' approach). In a more planned approach, tests supplement teacher-based identification in order to make the process more rigorous and less subjective. This is the point at which a school becomes preoccupied with tests and assessments. Many schools are, at this stage, seeking an ideal assessment tool to enable them to identify able children. Teachers are usually still thinking of their able children as a clearly defined group who have general ability in a variety of areas.

Tests and assessments are of course a vital part of the identification process but they can, in some schools, become the single form of identification. This is because it removes the need for the teacher to make professional decisions in an area where she or he does not feel confident. If the child does well on the test they must be able. This is probably in general terms a correct assumption but unfortunately the converse does not apply. It is perfectly possible for an able child to do badly on tests, for a variety of reasons. They may work slowly, be working in a second language, be unwilling to do repetitive tasks, be careless or exam-phobic. They may also 'out think' the test, looking for more complex answers than had been anticipated by the test designers. If you give a group of able children a standard multiple-choice question where they have to give the odd one out, they can usually justify a range of answers other than the expected one.

A second test constraint is in the type of tests used. As was amply demonstrated in Burgess' work, even a subject-based test may not test all elements of that particular subject. Most tests used in primary schools are linguistically based and are biased against children with other abilities and those who are working in a second language. Therefore tests must be used in full knowledge of their limitations and in conjunction with informed teacher assessment.

The search for an ideal test as a single method of identifying able children is futile. As staff move through this stage this may become apparent to them. However, some schools do choose to use tests as the basis of their selection of able children. This will lead to inaccurate and skewed identification and under-achievement. Other schools recognize the value of particular tests in supplementing their school-based assessment procedures and use them accordingly.

4. School-based systems

By this stage a school is beginning to understand that in order to identify ability effectively it will need to use a range of methods, each of which will contribute a particular type of information. The following are used by most schools:

- teacher nomination;
- tests and assessments – summative and diagnostic;
- checklists – general and subject-specific;
- educational psychologists;
- parental nomination;
- peer nomination;
- school awareness of the need to spot talent;
- identification through children's responses to challenging work.

All staff will, at this stage, be part of the discussion regarding the identification methods needed for their section of the school. Some methods are better suited to particular subjects, some to particular sorts of children, some to young children and some to older ones. A school at this stage should be confident enough to select a range of methods which suit its needs and circumstances. A predominately white middle-class school may rely more on standardized tests than a more ethnically mixed school. Reception classes may use observation more than Year 6.

At this stage teachers may still lack confidence in their own ability in the identification process. They are likely to have looked at general checklists and to be thinking more deeply about the characteristics of able children, but may still find it difficult to articulate their judgements.

5. A professional approach

This is the optimum stage in a school's progress towards effective identification. At this stage teachers are beginning to identify abilities with real confidence. Factors which may have led to this increase in teacher confidence are numerous. It is not possible to be prescriptive in defining a professional approach – it takes all the recommendations of stage 4 and adapts them in a way which makes the optimum use of staff expertise and the school's own situation; some of the sort of steps which schools might take as part of this approach are discussed below.

The school may have looked at identification on a subject-by-subject basis, identifying characteristics in each subject and those children exhibiting such characteristics. The school may have spent time looking at children's work, collecting a portfolio of examples and discussing their merits. One teacher of Year 5 and 6 collected three pieces of science work on circuits for the portfolio. When talking about them subsequently she concluded that only one of them was really outstanding. In the first piece of work the child had created a clown whose eyes lit up. This piece she described as very attractive but the actual science involved was quite simple. She had been beguiled by its attractive qualities and had failed to assess the science. In the second piece the work was tidy and well presented and she described it as a thorough execution of the task set; very good but not outstanding. In the third piece the child had used knowledge gained both in that lesson and from other sources to produce a more advanced circuit – a sign of real ability. This teacher was beginning to be able to make assessments with confidence and to recognize the characteristics of high achievement.

The school may also have spent time developing particular skills and techniques, for example observing children in the classroom to look for particular characteristics or behaviours. The work from Nebraska (Griffin et al., 1995) is a helpful basis for this. The whole staff may have, for a period, kept a log of interesting pupil comments or observations to develop their ability to recognize non-written indicators. All of these methods help individual teachers to gain a better professional understanding of able children and the type of work they need to do. Many of the characteristics of able children will only be observed if tasks are set which dictate their use. In Nebesnuick's work, one young teacher described a child as using higher order thinking. She must have set tasks which required higher order thinking for this ability to be observed.

In summary, a primary school will only be really effective in its identification of able children when all staff reach stage 5 of the process. In practice many schools stop at stages 2, 3 or 4. The school may think it is identifying its most able, but the process may be only partially effective or even ineffective. Stage 5 allows staff a development of identification skills and a greater understanding of the kinds of work which will need to be made available if such skills are to be fostered. This is why identification and provision are often described as two parts of a whole. Good provision allows a perceptive teacher to observe and recognize ability. A consideration of subject-specific abilities enables a teacher to see the types of work which need to be set.

Identification in the early years

An Oxfordshire LEA course run by their early years team was entitled, 'I think she may be bright'. This title sums up neatly the major issue in the identification of ability in young children: is what we are seeing now a true indicator of ability? It is well documented by Leyden (1985) and Freeman (1980) that some able children can be identified very early in their lives. These children tend to display a range of classic characteristics and are so unlike their peers that it would be difficult not to notice them. On a recent visit to a nursery school I noted the following:

> Marcus was in the nursery when I went to see him. He is an interesting child with a wonderful vocabulary and cheeky grin. He did not know that I was visiting him but soon came to find out what I was doing. I had been observing him and in my untidy handwriting had been making notes. He stood in front of me and read my notes perfectly from upside down and then asked if I would like to play with the telephone. The telephone in question has numbers which can be removed and replaced. Marcus played with the telephone by creating elaborate number patterns. He explained them as he went, even numbers, odd numbers, those which divide by three, etc. Everything about him was extraordinary. One could hardly fail to notice that he was very able.

Other children appear to be very able but may not be. A child who has a wide vocabulary and speaks confidently may come from a home where talk is highly valued and where opportunities for discussion are numerous. She or he could appear very able in the early years but as schooling progresses other children may begin to catch up. Equally, a child who writes or reads early may or may not go on to be an able reader or writer. It is tempting to take early signs of promise as clear indicators of ability. A more sensible approach may be to make appropriate provision for the child's needs at the time and monitor developments. This has implications for schools in that it may mean that an able child register, at least in Key Stage 1, is either inappropriate or subject to regular change.

An alternative system would be to consider those who in Key Stage 1 are in need of extension. This extension should be provided for as long as it is needed. Children who need extension change in the early years: some cease to make progress at the expected rate; others suddenly develop. Teachers of early years children sometimes fall into the trap of thinking of the older children, or those who have been in school the longest, as the most able. A period of six months is a long time in developmental terms at this age and younger children need to be judged according to their age rather than compared with older children in the same class.

In the early years children are most likely to be identified as able if they read or write early, if they speak confidently or if they are socially mature. More boys are identified than girls and more white middle-class children than those from other groups. Being aware of this bias, a good nursery or school should endeavour to be proactive in unearthing potential, rather than simply reacting to obvious signs of potential.

May appear able if:	*May be missed if:*
speaks confidently	English is the second language
mature	quiet
reads early	poor physical coordination
good motor skills	slow to read and write
born September/December	summer birthday
good general knowledge	little pre-school experience
has bright siblings	has slow siblings
attractive and lively.	scruffy and unappealing.

The following case study is an example of a school attempting to find a way to identify potential in the early years by observing the behaviour of children. The approach was developed in America by Griffin *et al.* (1995) and adapted for use in English schools as part of a research experiment. This work has a significance beyond the school in question because if it is an effective tool then it could be used by schools to identify potential in ethnically mixed or inner city schools. If potential can be observed through a child's behaviour then it should not matter if that child is working in a second language or is from a disadvantaged home. The child does not have to present in an accepted form in order to be recognized.

EARLY YEARS IDENTIFICATION AT
HOLYPORT CE PRIMARY SCHOOL

For many years we had looked for a suitable way to identify the able child in the early years. We had tried the various standard UK tests, but they tend to concentrate on academic aspects rather than the whole person and are inappropriate and/or culturally biased. You can, therefore, imagine our delight when attending the World Conference on Gifted and Talented Children in Toronto in the summer of 1993 to hear Dr Norma Sue Griffin talk about an identification procedure, based on observations rather than tests, which had been trialled and established in the State of Nebraska.

On our return to the UK a lengthy correspondence ensued followed by visits to the UK by Dr Griffin. It was eventually decided to replicate the Nebraska project in two large UK primary schools in the autumn and spring of 1994/5. Following the pilot, the findings were written up by two MA students and they make very interesting reading. The outcome was that our school has now adapted the Starry Night Observation Protocol as the primary means of identifying the able children in the nursery class. The main aim of the Nebraska Protocol, and our main aim, is to provide an unbiased and appropriate means of early identification of able children by their class teacher. Teachers are given a better understanding of the child's behaviour and learning preferences in order to guide and influence the creation of an optimal learning environment. The Protocol is not intended to categorise children by label or ability group or to fast track. It does, however, offer a reference point for measuring value-added performance. It is designed to 'change the learning landscape for able children during their early school years'.

The Protocol identifies a wide range of behaviours, including the usual well-recognised ones such as early reading or advanced mathematical ability. The wide range of behaviours so identified fits well with the 'gifts into talents' theory, as developed by Gagné (1994), which is an important part of our school policy on able children. The Protocol uses the term 'Starry Night' to emphasise the non-cultural, non-traditional, but nonetheless authentic, nature of this assessment instrument. There are 17 constellations in the Starry Night or 17 behaviour patterns to be observed:

- ACT HUNGER: expressive, role play, show, exhibit, gesture, spontaneous, lead, announce, enthusiastic
- CURIOUS – QUESTIONS: notices, examines, observes, seeks/asks, requests, has insight/connects
- ENGAGES: initiates, directs/leads, attracts, encourages, shows how, offers or extends instruction/help
- EXPLORES: experiments, pretends, builds, designs, constructs, organises/sorts, solves, plays
- FANTASY – IMAGINATION: invents, imitates, imagines, pretends, original construction, novel design
- FOCUS: absorbed, diligent, concentrates, organises/sorts, completes detail
- HUMOUR: jokes, clever, original, spontaneous, notices/creates, reacts/responds
- IMAGERY: uses metaphors, detects, symbolism, illustrates, artistic, clever, novel, original, expressive
- INDEPENDENT: works alone, self-directed, initiates, absorbed, diligent, concentrates, plans/pursues/solves
- KNOWS: comprehends/reasons, connects/associates, finds/applies/uses, answers/announces, explains, calculates/solves
- MOVING AND DOING: demonstrates, constructs, looks/reacts, shows how or what, exhibits, non-verbal expressive
- OBSERVANT: notices, sees relation, connects/associates/predicts, examines, distinguishes, determines (sees) differences (change)
- RECOGNISED (BY OTHERS): sought out, seen as a resource, shows how, helps, attracts others (as magnet), responsive, admired
- SEES THE BIG PICTURE: recognises pattern, comprehends, associates, finds metaphor, predicts, analyses/theorises
- SENSITIVE: expressive/quick to tear, insightful, thoughtful, helpful, sympathetic/empathetic, anxious, self-aware, concern/care
- SHARES – VOLUNTEERS: extends (to others), illustrates, connects/describes, explains/instructs, helps/shows how, advises, encourages
- VOCABULARY: fluent, comprehends, express/expressive, novel, associates/connects, complex syntax, uses 'big' words

plus

- COMET: any behaviour that is 'off-the-wall' or spectacular and cannot be ignored as evidence of special ability but does not appear to fall into other categories.

During the pilot project we had long debates about the American language used for some behaviours, in particular 'act hunger' and 'sees the big picture', but in the end we decided that we could not actually improve the terminology. It is interesting to note that 'sees the big picture' has become part of the school vocabulary.

So how does the identification actually work? In a child's second half-term in the nursery class, the staff will observe the children over a 15-day period and record any comments made by a child or any observations of behaviour, play patterns, etc., that are above the norm. These are then categorised into one or more of the constellations, recorded on an individual record sheet [see Figure 2.5] and then analysed.

The outcome of the analysis is used to place the child into one of four categories:

- the verbal knowing independent child,
- the curious moving and doing explorer child,
- the quiet focused unexpectedly humorous child,
- the socially interactive engaging 'on stage' child.

These four types of child perform best in different environments and their learning styles need to be taken into consideration when planning classroom activities. The staff now take these preferred learning styles into account when they are doing their short term planning.

The great advantage of this procedure is that it can be undertaken in the classroom during normal routines; the observations can be done by the nursery teacher and the nursery nurse. The number of children identified using this method is approximately 12–15% of the cohort. Unlike the more traditional methods of identification the Nebraska Protocol encourages staff to look and to 'see the big picture'.

Johanna Raffan, Headteacher

A final issue in respect of identification in the early years relates to the link between baseline assessment and early identification of ability. The move in the 1990s towards baseline assessment procedures has been the result of both political and professional pressures, the desire to create an appropriate early years curriculum and at the same time ensure a seamless entry into National Curriculum work. From the perspective of able children it has been a considerable move forward. Prior to this, few schools asked for information on learning experiences or paid much attention to profiling a child's pre-school cognitive development. This has, in the past, led to low expectations of able children in the early years. Assessments based on observation, checklists or performance on structured tasks all allow able children to demonstrate their capabilities. This should facilitate better match on entry into school.

A note of caution is needed here, however, because some assessment activities are based on a can/cannot achieve approach to particular tasks, e.g. follow simple instructions and name and describe familiar objects. This type of assessment does not allow for children who achieve at a level significantly beyond the expected. What about the child who can already follow complex instructions or who not only knows the colours but can spell them all too? A space needs to be included on such sheets for unexpected levels of performance, otherwise a true assessment will not have been made.

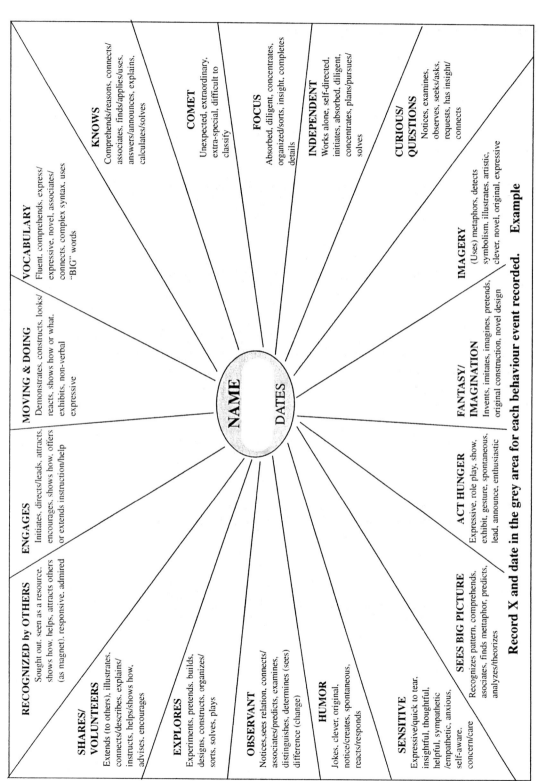

Figure 2.5 Nebraska Starry Night: individual record sheet

Able children with special educational needs

The Code of Practice on the Identification and Assessment of Special Educational Needs (DfEE, 1994) identifies eight categories of children with special educational needs. It is important to remember that able pupils can be identified under at least half of these categories.

Specific learning difficulties (dyslexic able children)

This is perhaps the category of special need most often linked to able children. Many dyslexic children are able or very able and may well be on a school's able child register as well as the special needs register. Children who have been diagnosed as dyslexic may be assisted in accessing higher level and extension tasks using appropriate technology. Their dyslexia should not lead to a lowering of expectations but rather a focus on enabling performance. A significant number of children, especially boys, seem to be very able but have problems with recording information in writing. This may be a mild form of dyslexia or another problem entirely. Since no research into this group of pupils has been undertaken there are no definitive findings.

Physical disabilities and sensory impairments

This is another under-researched area. Children identified as having special needs in the physical disabilities or sensory impairment categories may also be very able. Once again the challenge comes in enabling access to higher level tasks. In the case of some physical disabilities this may be linked to general access issues, such as use of equipment in specialist teaching areas like science laboratories, etc. In the case of children with sight loss or coordination problems there is sometimes a difficulty with the materials available to facilitate access. These tend to be pitched at a low level and may not present the kinds of challenges needed. An exceptionally able Year 3 child in mainstream school has cerebral palsy. His speech is slow and his coordination poor. He uses the computer with an adapted keyboard. However, the materials available to help children with his kind of coordination problems do not expect children to be working at his level. The kinds of sentences he wants to use are complex and the information he wants to convey is detailed and sophisticated. Voice-operated equipment may help, but the frustration for him is immense.

Emotional and behavioural difficulties

A surprising number of children who are identified by schools in this category are also very able. There is a clear link here between good curriculum provision and behaviour. For some children school has just been too dull and boring. Many able children find repetitive tasks difficult and some will simply refuse to do them. The classic example here is Monday morning news. Able children like to see a purpose to the activities they undertake and often view news as both pointless and uninteresting. Therefore they may refuse to do it. In Key Stage 1 refusal to do work is a not infrequent response from some able children.

By Key Stage 2 this pattern of behaviour is often set. Able children who do not like or value school can be highly disruptive if they set their mind to it. They are good planners and can judge the points of maximum impact and often organize others to assist them in disruptive behaviour. They may be very able but cannot settle to work and need the same short-term manageable goals as others with behaviour problems. It often seems incongruous that a child with high intellectual ability is unable to recognize the implications of his or her behaviour. However, intellectual and emotional development are quite different things and it is possible to be very able and at the same time emotionally immature.

The secondary school can sometimes be the final straw for highly individualistic able children. The primary school may have allowed for their individuality but the secondary timetable is too rigid in its expectations for the child to conform. Their academic performance declines and along with it their behaviour.

Schools generally seem to be rather intolerant of able children with emotional problems; they see them as having the ability but not choosing to use it. For example, they are much less tolerant than they might be of a child who misbehaves because they find the work too difficult. Given that many able children, of all varieties, allude to the large percentage of their schooling which leaves them under-challenged and unfulfilled, it is hardly surprising that a percentage of these children choose to become disruptive. A focus on provision for able children may well solve some of a school's behaviour problems.

Identification: conclusions

Identification is without doubt an important but also troublesome area in the education of able pupils. Headteachers and senior managers should not make assumptions about the expertise of staff in this area but should recognize the likelihood of a lack of confidence and provide appropriate support and training. The key messages regarding identification are summarized below.

1. Definition and identification are closely linked

A school cannot begin to look at methods of identification until all staff are agreed on the definitions to be used. If, for example, the definition adopted is to be a broad one which includes musical, sporting, artistic and other creative abilities, then clearly the identification methods cannot solely be linked to school exams and progress tests. Defining the cohort is the first stage in the identification process.

2. Testing alone cannot provide the answer

Exhaustive attempts have been made to devise tests that identify particular abilities. These tests provide useful information but they are not infallible. Teachers generally tend to want to use, and rely on, tests as their major method of identification. However, research indicates that such tests may be inaccurate, especially blanket tests that are given to all pupils. These become increasingly unreliable at either extreme of the ability range. Children may 'out think' the test or under-perform due to the linguistic bias of the tests.

3. Able pupils are not a clearly defined group

Assuming that a school is seeking to nurture a wide range of abilities, then the idea of a clearly defined group of able pupils will be erroneous. The good footballer may not be academic; those with good leadership and interpersonal skills may not excel in other areas. The school needs to decide whether any register of able pupils is to be restricted to those who show ability across a range of subjects or is to include all those who show outstanding ability in any curriculum area. (As suggested by Denton and Postlethwaite [1985] and confirmed by later studies, approximately 40 per cent of the pupils in an average comprehensive school come in the top 10 per cent in one subject.) Some schools create a group based on ability in, say, six subject areas. However, it is worth remembering that Einstein would not have made the able pupils group using this criterion.

4. Some abilities may not be recognized until later in a pupil's schooling

Some indicators of ability are clearly recognizable when a child transfers from primary to secondary school, others are not. Obviously, ability in the new curriculum areas, like modern languages, may not be apparent, and it may take some time for these to be recognizable. In some subjects, e.g. history, personal maturity is needed before outstanding ability is recognizable. Even in the case of subjects that have been taught throughout primary school, the introduction of specialist teaching can lead to a new enthusiasm and uncovering of latent ability.

5. Ability and achievement are not the same thing

Schools have a vital role to play in providing the opportunities and support needed to help pupils maximize their potential. Innate ability is, at best, a factor in achievement. From a school's perspective, it is important to spot those pupils who may have significant potential as well as those who are already converting that into performance. An identification system may therefore need to 'code' able under-achievers as well as able achievers.

6. Opportunities and motivation make a difference

Much recent research stresses the importance of personal motivation in high achievement. Therefore, a school system must not dwell on an elite at the expense of others. Effort must be highly valued but opportunities too are important. When identifying groups for special attention through enrichment and extension, a school should give motivation equal status with achievement.

7. Identification and classroom provision

The main purpose of identifying able pupils is to improve classroom provision. Any system that fails to lead to this outcome is ineffective. There is nothing to be gained by trying to measure ability very accurately; what matters is that where ability exists it is recognized and nurtured. All teachers need to know what they are looking for and when they have found it.

Chapter 3

A Differentiated Approach to Classroom Planning

Introduction

This chapter looks in some detail at ways to develop differentiated planning techniques for use in the classroom. The ideas are equally useful in setted or mixed ability groupings and can be applied to a variety of subjects. Examples are drawn from both the primary and secondary sector and many of the ideas are equally applicable to both. Additional information which is particularly pertinent to each phase of education can be found in Chapters 4 and 5.

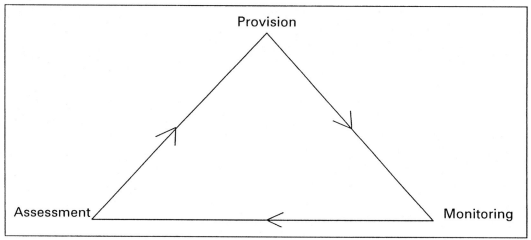

Figure 3.1 The differentiation process

In order to make effective provision for individuals the teacher needs to be involved in a continuous cycle of assessment, planning and monitoring: assessing the particular needs of individuals, attempting to provide appropriately and monitoring the result. The monitoring findings then provide the starting point for new assessment and planning.

This process has sometimes been referred to as differentiation. Differentiation is of course a crucial aspect of good provision for the most able. Able children are likely to need at least some modification to the standard expected outcome for a lesson and in the case of very able or exceptional children this might be a significant deviation from the norm. In planning terms a teacher may be thinking of a range of expected outcomes from the class, reflecting their different strengths and abilities. She may be setting tasks or giving support in such a way as to *enable* children to reach different outcomes. This approach has particular significance since in some classrooms the emphasis on all children meeting a minimum standard has led to inappropriately low levels of achievement from the most able.

Differentiation has been the focus of much attention in the educational world. Teachers have been exhorted to take a differentiated approach to learning and teaching but guidance on how to achieve this has been limited. In terms of a definition we could say:

Differentiation is…
recognizing individual differences and trying to find institutional strategies which take account of them.

Schools need…
a workable system which is flexible enough to accommodate individual need.

Much of the existing literature on differentiation is highly mechanistic in its approach and is limited in its usefulness as far as provision for the most able is concerned. Differentiation by task, outcome, resource and support are a feature of differentiated provision for the most able, but alone they do not address the subtleties of good provision. Differentiation by outcome, for example, can in practice refer to a range of experiences. At its most basic level it can simply mean setting the same task for everyone and expecting a range of different outcomes which relate directly to the abilities of the pupils involved. However the 'outcome' can be affected, and indeed greatly enhanced, by teacher intervention. The 'Have you thought about…' kind of comment can change the outcome significantly and lead to the child moving into a new and higher level of thinking.

In this chapter the intention is to consider differentiation particularly from the perspective of able children: how classroom planning and teaching can be structured to extend pupils, and the general principles which underpin good provision. However, since in ordinary schools provision for the most able is usually part of general classroom planning, the approaches used in this chapter build on a teacher's existing planning rather than look at the most able in isolation. This is a significant departure from most writing in this field, which has historically been restricted to optimizing effective provision for the most able without attempting to consider the manageability of such provision within the context of the ordinary classroom.

This chapter draws upon the work of a variety of researchers into provision for able pupils, for example Gallagher, Montgomery, Bloom, Renzulli *et al.,* and shows how aspects of their approaches can successfully be incorporated into general classroom planning. It also considers a variety of interesting teaching ideas, such as Robert Fisher's Thinking Skills work, Aiden Chambers' 'Book Talk' and Lunzer and Gardner's Directed Activities Related to Text (DARTS), and shows how these can be utilized to provide extension work for the most able. Finally, this chapter draws on the extensive body of action research undertaken by the author with Oxfordshire schools, and aims to provide a blueprint for schools seeking to improve their classroom provision for the most able.

Differentiation: where should it occur and what does it look like?

One reason why differentiation is so difficult to tackle is because opportunities for differentiation occur at all levels within school and in both planned and unplanned situations. Fast tracking is a form of differentiation; so too is setting and the provision of coaching opportunities for sport; similarly, instrumental music tuition and school clubs and societies. Each represents different provision to meet the needs of individuals.

In practice all teachers differentiate at least to some extent. What we are seeking to do is to increase or improve differentiation. It is not possible to differentiate for all children all the time – true differentiation is an aspiration – however, that does not negate the need to strive for improvement.

Differentiation: planning and opportunism

Most of this chapter will focus on planning for greater differentiation but it should be noted that not all differentiation actually happens as a result of planning. Some good differentiation is the result of 'opportunism'. This occurs when a teacher sees an unplanned opportunity present itself within the lesson and builds on it. Such opportunities may be the result of a question or comment from a pupil or from the outcome or results of work. Either way the teacher may deviate from the planned lesson to take advantage of the opportunity to move children forward in their thinking, either individually or collectively. Such opportunities are of immense value because they build on a child's interest and motivation to strive for understanding of a particularly difficult concept or idea.

In the case of the most able, teachers who can take advantage of opportunism are likely to see outstanding work. Able pupils often glimpse an idea beyond what is being addressed in class but need a little help or, as Vygotsky would term it, 'scaffolding' to enable them to move forward in their thinking. There does seem to be a clear link here between a thorough understanding of the subject being taught and the ability of the teacher to maximize such opportunities. It is very difficult for a teacher to take advantage of a pupil's tangential interest when teaching a subject with which she or he is either unfamiliar or under-confident. In my research with Mary Fuller (Eyre and Fuller, 1993), teachers expressed themselves as being less willing to deviate from their planning in areas of the curriculum where they lacked confidence. Their planning provided a safe, secure environment with which they could cope. Pupils who asked difficult questions made the teacher feel de-skilled and were sometimes resented. This problem is not restricted to primary schools but is also common in secondary schools where teachers have been given subjects to teach which are not their specialisms.

Since the advent of the National Curriculum and monitoring of its delivery, teachers have become more reluctant to deviate from their plans. When working recently with a first school, one of the teachers described a lesson on the compass which had gone unexpectedly well. One child had, unprompted, recognized the link between the compass points and right angles. The teacher explained that she did not feel able to address this issue within the lesson because right angles did not occur in the plans for that term. This kind of inflexibility is highly detrimental to the most able. Curiosity cannot be put back in a box and revisited later, especially not where young children are concerned.

The National Curriculum is a mechanism for ensuring that all pupils cover key content and concepts, it should not become a straitjacket which restricts the creativity of pupils and their teachers.

Opportunism is not, however, a substitute for planning. Some teachers take the view that if they know what they want to cover in the lesson then they will be able to intervene with the most able to take them further when and if the opportunity occurs. This might be termed 'ad hoc differentiation'. Unfortunately, while this sounds beguiling in theory, it has limited effectiveness is practice. Invariably the extension needs either resources which are not in the classroom or ideas which do not readily spring to mind. If, for example, the extension involved the child in making a comparison between the class text and another similar text then (a) it might not be easy to think immediately of another suitable text and (b) that text is unlikely to be in the classroom.

Therefore opportunism and planning should go hand-in-hand. Sometimes the teacher will deviate from the planning to respond to the interest of pupils. This may be added to the planning retrospectively. It may even be that the opportunistic departure was so successful that it becomes part of the planning next time that lesson is taught. Equally, the planning for a lesson may recognize that the most appropriate form of differentiation is, in this instance, through intervention with individuals. In this case it may be noted in the planning documents in the extension column. One advantage of making such a note is that it ensures that the lesson is planned in such a way as to make time for such interventions. Research shows (Eyre and Fuller, 1993) that whilst teachers often intend to intervene with individuals, in reality the time is often eroded by the need to address classroom management issues. Therefore, careful planning is needed if such an approach is to be used.

Including extension in classroom planning

Extension planning or categories can be added to any of the familiar existing planning methods.

1. Must, should, could

This is an incremental method in which everyone covers a core content and then moves on as far as they are able. Used sensitively this can work well with able pupils. They will often cover the core very quickly and move on to more extending work. The greatest advantage of this method is that the route forward is clearly identified and decisions about who does what can be made on the basis of achievement on the task. If a pupil does well on the 'must' and 'should' they will be encouraged to move onto the 'could'. The teacher does not need to

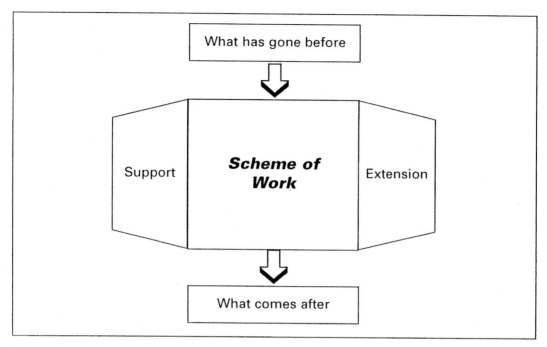

Figure 3.2 Howard's planning model

identify an extension group at the beginning. The major limitations lie in the need to start at the core, and for slow workers. Some extremely able children work very slowly and are reluctant to move on until they have explored and reconciled in their own mind all aspects of each element of the task. These pupils are capable of undertaking the 'could' but are often found languishing in the 'must' section.

2. Skills, concepts, content, resources

This popular model uses a series of columns to show skills, concepts, content and resources. Its strength lies in its clear layout and easy link with National Curriculum requirements. The difficulty is that it can easily lead to everyone doing the same task or tasks in the same way. However, it can easily be adapted to include differentiation. This can be done either by showing extension targets in all columns, e.g. additional skills, concepts and knowledge, or by adding an extension column which illustrates how the initial planning will be adapted for the most able.

The model for extension planning

In thinking about extension planning there are two major considerations in addition to actual content or task design: first, how the extension relates to general class provision and second, how to pitch the extension at an appropriate level. Continuity and progression are just as important in extension planning as in all other planning. Bolt-on, one-off extension ideas are of limited value and effectiveness.

Therefore any model for provision should incorporate both of these elements. The diagram shown in Figure 3.2 was the work of my colleague Richard Howard (Senior Inspector, Oxfordshire LEA) and has much to commend it. It is very simple and can be applied to all subjects and to all ages. It makes extension (and support) a natural part of all planning and builds on children's existing knowledge, skills and understanding. It is an excellent way of thinking about extension planning and I have used it extensively with schools in Oxfordshire and elsewhere.

Who should do extension?

When considering differentiation for the most able it is helpful to think about who will do the extension work. This is actually a more complex question than it might at first appear. An instinctive response would be to identify the most able and give them the extension work. Of course the 'most able' group would vary according to the subject and perhaps to the nature of the task, so data would need to be available regarding pupils' achievements in all subjects and in all types of task. Even then the issue of opportunity would be neglected. If the teacher always chooses the extension group then there is little opportunity for the supposedly average child to display unexpected flair or ability. The system is neat and tidy but limited.

A more effective approach is to use a variety of methods for deciding who does extension and allow the task to dictate the method used. Each method has its place. Sometimes the criterion for undertaking extension work will be speed, sometimes ability, sometimes choice. What is important is that no one method is used exclusively. Some children, for example, would never choose to do harder work, even though they are quite capable. They may suffer from low self-esteem and not be aware of their ability, or they may simply be lazy and opt to do as little as possible.

The most effective way to handle extension work is to plan the activity or task first, and then decide who in the class could tackle it.

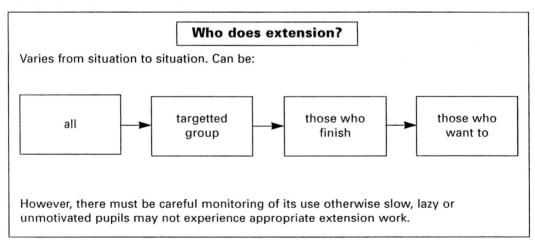

Figure 3.3 Who does extension?

Methods of establishing a starting point (diagnostic assessment)

A common mistake when planning extension work is for the teacher to make assumptions regarding the pupils' current level of understanding or knowledge about a subject. Able pupils often complain of having to start at the beginning of a module or topic even though they already know a good deal about it. It is very tempting to assume that if the knowledge or concepts have not been taught in school then pupils will be unfamiliar with them. In practice some able pupils may have extensive knowledge. If extension work is to be at all successful in a crowded curriculum, we must become more skilled at establishing appropriate starting points for children rather than assuming that everyone will start in the same place. Of course, we need to be clear that pupils have a robust understanding of any concepts or skills which are to be 'skipped', otherwise gaps in understanding can occur. Able pupils, like all others, do need to be taught skills. However, they usually need to practise them less than other children.

The National Curriculum was intended to facilitate individual progress with an acceptance that pupils will achieve at a variety of levels. In practice, however, the strong emphasis on accountability which has accompanied the National Curriculum has made many teachers over-cautious when dealing with able pupils. The desire to demonstrate that all children have covered the required content, concepts and skills has, in some cases, led to an emphasis on teaching at the expense of learning: a preoccupation with what pupils are being given to do rather than what they are learning. Identified outcomes for pupils' learning are not always a feature of short-term planning and certainly additional outcomes for the most able are rare.

How then can a teacher decide where to pitch the module or lesson generally, and also where to pitch the extension work? There are a whole range of methods available to help in this decision, from the informal to the very formal. Some lend themselves more readily to some subjects than others, some to particular age groups. Indeed which methods are used may be influenced by the teacher's own preferred style of working.

What is important is that accrediting prior learning becomes a feature of the assessment, provision, monitoring process.

Some methods for establishing a starting point are:

- 'carpet time' or classroom questions
- class brainstorm
- setting an open task
- concept mapping
- quiz
- pre-test or assessment
- building on existing evidence.

1. 'Carpet time' or classroom questions

This is the most informal method of obtaining information regarding children's prior knowledge. Usually it starts with the teacher asking, 'Who can tell me anything about…'. Often this is followed by a silence until someone offers a tentative response which triggers everyone else's thinking, e.g.:

Teacher: Who can tell me anything about the Egyptians?

Child: Did they have mummies?

After this a number of children will add information and the class are often surprised to find how much they know already.

In a secondary classroom offers may be less forthcoming for a number of reasons. It may not be culturally acceptable to be seen as clever and therefore even those who have something to contribute may not choose to share it. Some adolescents are also less willing to face the potential embarrassment of being wrong and so are unwilling to speculate. So, this approach, if used in the secondary school, may need adaptation. It may be best suited to setted groups. It may be helpful to ask pupils to work in pairs or threes so that any observations are not theirs alone. It may, in the end, prove not to be a useful method for secondary pupils.

2. Class brainstorm

This is a popular extension of the above idea. It also has certain advantages. First, because ideas are being generated in rapid succession, the question of being wrong is somehow less acute. Second, the process of committing the information to paper allows pupils to revisit it at later stages of the module. This helps some children to obtain a better understanding of the relationship between different aspects of the module. In some primary classrooms such a brainstorm becomes an integral part of the topic, with children adding to it as they discover new things. This idea could easily be adapted for use in secondary schools, with each pupil creating his or her own module web for particular modules of work.

3. Setting an open task

For a fast, easy method of assessing current levels of understanding it is possible to set an open task and note the nature of the response. This can be done in a variety of ways and at the start or finish of a module. One way is to ask an open question or give pupils a copy of a picture.

School example 1

In the reception class the teacher asked children to make up questions for which the answer is 10. Most children worked on adding, many using the multi-link maths equipment. Marcus covered addition, subtraction and multiplication and was also able to generalize about the patterns he was seeing.

School example 2

Daniel's class had just finished a topic looking at what does and does not conduct electricity. The task for his group was to come up with some questions about electricity to which they did not know the answer (see Figure 3.4). Clearly, especially in question 10, Daniel demonstrates an understanding beyond what might reasonably be expected. The Science Curriculum for KS1 suggests that children should be able to 'Relate simple scientific ideas to the evidence for them'; I would suggest that it is unlikely that the writers were anticipating a response at Daniel's level.

Questions

1. How can water conduct electricity?
2. Does metal or water conduct electricity best?
3. Metal conducts electricity. Does brass?
4. Do metal things with plastic in them conduct electricity?
5. Does a paint can with paint in it conduct electricity?
6. Does wire conduct electricity?
7. Would a black-board with metal stands conduct electricity?
8. If you conneted a 10v battery and wires to a sheet of meatal, and put 5x2 wires also on it all leading to 2v bulbs, would it blow the bulbs or would the bulbs conduct the right amount of energy?
9. Does copper conduct electricity?
10. If wood doesn't conduct electricity, how come there are trees that are struck by

lightening?

Daniel Taylor, Year 2, Scientist.

Figure 3.4 Daniel's questions on electricity

School example 3

What could you say about the picture shown in Figure 3.5? Obviously responses to this can vary from the simplistic to the highly complex.

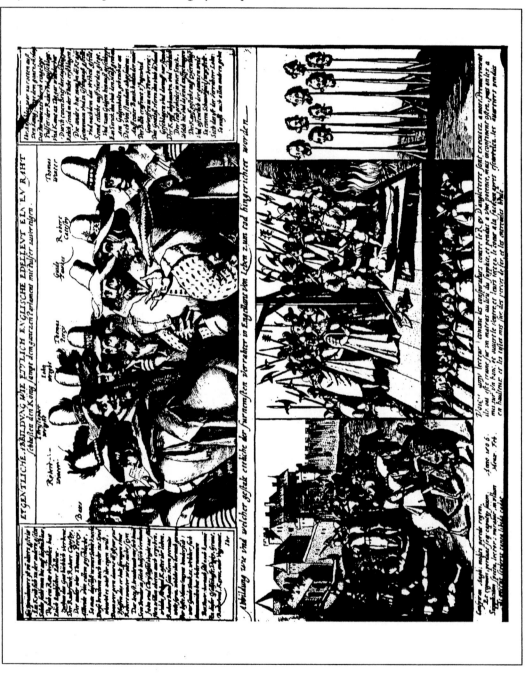

Figure 3.5 The Gunpowder Plot: picture used to asess existing knowledge

4. Concept mapping

This approach, devised by Tony Buzan (1995), encourages pupils to categorize their thoughts in a logical way, so assisting memory. It is particularly helpful in assisting secondary pupils who need to remember information for exams, but it has many other uses. It is in some ways like a topic web, but emphasizes the conceptual links between ideas and information. Therefore it is a useful way of assessing conceptual understanding.

If concept mapping is taught at an early stage, children become increasingly good at it. Able pupils often find it particularly appealing, especially those who do not like writing. From the assessment point of view it can be used at the start of a module to assess current understanding, or at the end of the module. A rewarding way to use it is at both the start and the end, so allowing the pupil to see the progress made. Once children have become familiar with the technique it is possible to ask individuals or groups to construct a concept map so enabling an assessment of their understanding. Although this technique was originally devised for adults it can easily be used with children as young as Year 5 and 6, and some teachers have even used it in KS1 with a little support and guidance. Some children find concept mapping a very useful way to work and use it extensively.

The Year 6 example shown in Figure 3.6 is very interesting as an end-of-module example. The class had covered three main aspects of the Tudors: Henry VIII and Elizabeth I, medicine and health care, and houses and homes. Clearly the latter did not impinge very much on this child's consciousness.

5. Quiz

Another possible way to assess current understanding is the use of a quiz. This can cover key information or concepts or both. It is useful to remember here that pictures or cartoons can be used equally as effectively as words and are often more appealing to pupils. A useful idea for able pupils is to ask them, at the end of a module or topic, to design a quiz for next year's group. This requires some quite high level thinking (synthesis) on the part of the designers and has the added advantage of cutting down on future teacher planning.

6. Pre-test or assessment

This technique can provide clear data on pupil performance at either the start or the end of the module. It lends itself particularly well to subjects where the knowledge and concepts to be covered are clearly defined, such as science modules. An effective way to use this is with pupils as part of their self-assessment. Schools which have a tradition of pupil self-evaluation, through Records of Achievement or similar, find that the judgements made by pupils are generally accurate and can give information of high quality. As far as able pupils are concerned this approach has two specific advantages. First, it gives them the opportunity to demonstrate mastery of some concepts at the start of the module, so avoiding repetition of work already understood. Second, it allows pupils to see the form and structure of the module to be covered. This facilitates greater independence and may lead to some pupils exploring aspects of the module in their own time, prior to coverage in class. High standards are frequently achieved when able pupils are enabled to take some control of their own learning, and access to the 'learning agenda' for the module is a prerequisite for this.

48

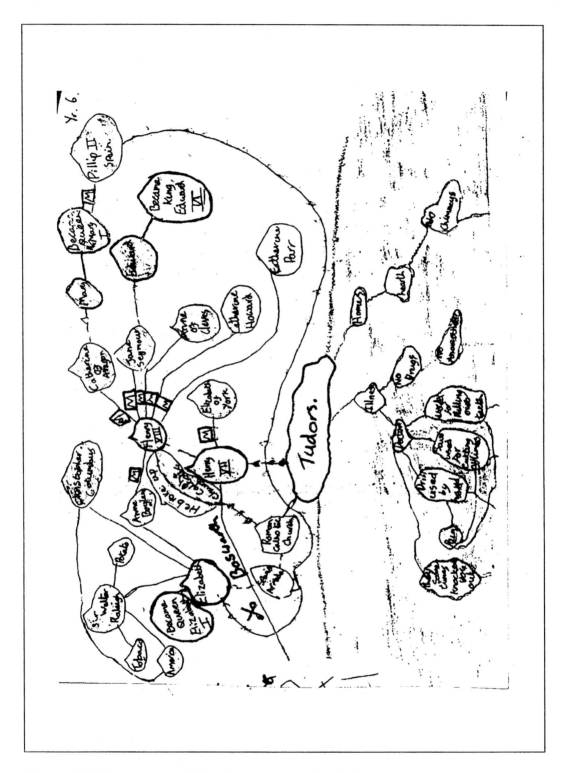

Figure 3.6 Concept map, following work on the Tudors

In the example shown in Figure 3.7, aspects of this Year 8 module are already understood by the pupil. Others parts are partially understood and some areas are completely unfamiliar.

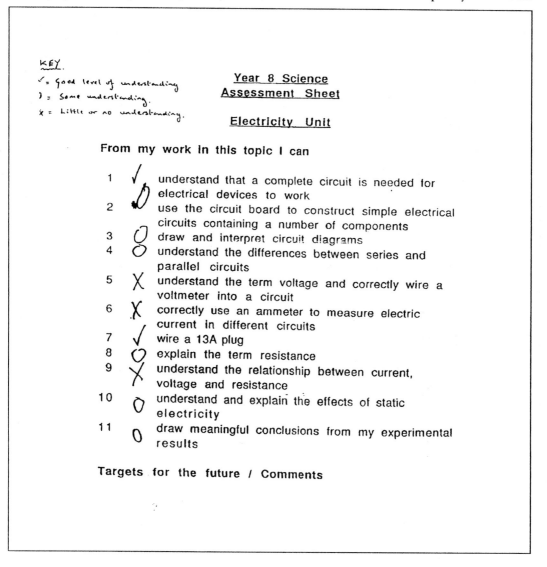

Figure 3.7 Example of a Year 8 science self-assessment

7. Building on existing evidence

This should of course be the basis of much of the school's assessment practice. In reality a large proportion of assessment in schools is summative and concerned with whether a pupil does or does not understand particular skills, concepts and knowledge. This kind of approach, while useful in assessing minimum standards, is unhelpful for able pupils because it does not allow them to demonstrate mastery beyond the expected. Not only can they do what is being asked, they could do much more. Therefore, if a school is to be effective in its extension planning it must consider previous evidence of achievement. This will usually be part of the school's assessment process and may include personal portfolios of work or evidence from particular assessed activities.

The extension targets in some tasks may therefore be specifically related to performance on previous similar tasks.

Figure 3.8 shows a letter written by Catherine, who is in Year 1. She wrote the letter unaided. When the class are being taught letter writing, what would be an appropriate extension task for Catherine?

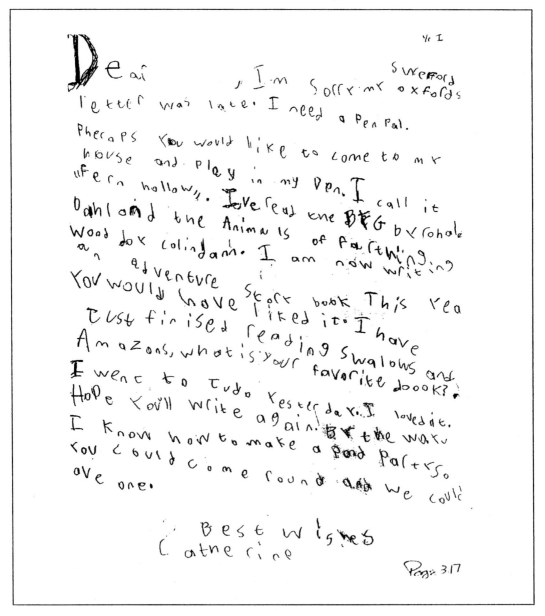

Figure 3.8 Catherine's work (Year 1)

Summary

A key principle in planning differentiated work for the most able is an informed appreciation of current levels of achievement and understanding. There are a wide variety of ways in which such information can be gained and these could usefully be explored at departmental or school level. If the school is seeking to improve its differentiation for the most able then it needs to be clear about the way existing school assessment structures can facilitate extension planning and also about other diagnostic assessment methods which could be incorporated into classroom or departmental planning. Extension should not assume that all pupils are starting from the same place.

Teaching and learning styles

Much has been written on the need to employ a variety of teaching styles. In my work on teaching styles I have found that in practice most teachers use a limited range of styles which they have found to be effective, and occasionally adopt an additional style for a particular purpose. Personal choice of styles is influenced by the subject being taught but perhaps more by the teacher's preferred approach to the subject. When this issue is discussed as part of whole-school INSET, different departments frequently identify particular styles as being well suited to their subject. They assert that they would use a wider range of styles but are restricted by subject-appropriateness. This argument would have greater credibility if the same styles were identified by the same departments in all the schools I visit. In reality, while some styles do emerge as particularly useful for some subjects, other styles can be used if required.

In respect of able pupils it is tempting to assume that particular styles are best suited to the most able. In practice all have specific advantages and disadvantages. Below, I discuss some teaching and learning styles:

1. open-ended tasks for all
2. workrate
3. tasks by ability group
4. starting from the core
5. individually negotiated tasks
6. core plus options.

1. Open-ended task for all

This is by far the easiest method to plan and has the advantage of allowing the most able to be fully integrated in the class. It is particularly well suited to English teaching where the teacher may intervene with particular pupils to discuss individual targets as they work. The major disadvantages from the point of view of the most able are threefold. First, the task may be set at a level which is inappropriately low. This is often dependent on the nature of the class cohort. It is unlikely to be a problem in a setted class or where a number of able pupils exist within the class, but can be a major problem in mixed ability classes and in primary classes where the mean of the class is low. It is interesting to note here that in many secondary school this method is used extensively in mixed ability English groups.

A second problem with this method relates to the assumption that all pupils will do their best work and the most able will achieve most highly. This is accurate for some able pupils but by no means all. Some are not highly motivated and will produce only a minimum. Some find this approach too open-ended. They need a little more structure if they are to excel. This is a characteristic of a whole category of able pupils. They can achieve highly but need assistance in determining how to begin and to structure a task.

The third problem relates to timing. This style of teaching often asks pupils to do their best in the time available. This can be frustrating for the most able who identify a more complex response to the task and may need longer to develop it. Equally, if no time-scale is identified, as sometimes happens in primary schools, then some able pupils lose focus and pace.

2. Workrate

This applies to working through a scheme or exercise. Differentiation is by workrate in that the questions become progressively more difficult. This is used most frequently in maths, at secondary school through SMP maths and at primary through commercial schemes. The advantages to the approach are linked to the child being able to progress at their own rate without having to wait for others. Clearly this is particularly important for able pupils. An additional benefit lies in the clearly identified progression route which makes it well suited to a linear subject like maths.

Disadvantages are linked to motivation and fragmentation. Such schemes assume that the most able will work through the scheme most rapidly, so keeping their work well matched to their achievement level. Most pupils do, but a significant number of able pupils become out of step with the scheme. They may be slow perfectionists, or they may be demotivated and intimidated by the never-ending nature of such work. Seeing the route forward from book one to book six can be highly motivating for some able pupils and give them a real feeling of control; for others it equates to a jail sentence and actively slows their workrate. Such approaches may also be limited in terms of the thinking required from pupils and can convert maths into a highly mechanistic procedure.

Class fragmentation can also occur when too much work is reliant on workrate. Because able pupils can generally complete the work set, they often are left for long periods to complete exercises or booklets with no opportunity for discussion regarding the learning taking place. This very passive approach does not tend to encourage real enjoyment of a subject or intellectual excitement. This limitation is not restricted to maths but is also a feature of computer-integrated learning systems.

3. Tasks by ability group

This teaching style can be well suited to able pupils. My own research suggests that able pupils are more likely to set tasks which really challenge them if they are grouped by ability. This is because the starting point for the task will be higher. This style can be used in all subjects, and can add an additional dimension to a subject which frequently uses other methods, for example English.

Disadvantages are social and organizational. Socially, too much use of ability grouping can lead to an elite emerging. This happens particularly when grouping does not change from subject to subject. A small group is constantly recognized as being the most able, and this can adversely affect others in the class. At secondary level this is done through streaming or grammar schools.

The second problem area with this approach relates to the creation of or selection for groups or sets. Often this is very crude and potentially able pupils can find themselves excluded. In secondary schools sets are often created based on performance in tests and take no account of underachievers, and in primary school on the assessment of a single teacher. Selection is sometimes the result of a confusion between high quality thinking and neat, tidy working, with the latter children making the top group.

4. Starting from the core

This is a highly inclusive approach in that all pupils do some core tasks and then, based on their performance, they may move on to other tasks. The 'must, should, could' planning approach uses this teaching style. For able pupils this works well, except for slow or tentative workers who may need encouragement to access the higher levels.

This style can also be used in whole-class teaching with the teacher juggling or managing the progress of individuals within the context of a shared agenda. This style is less effective for able pupils if the core is set at a low level or if the majority of time is spent on the core activities.

5. Individually negotiated tasks

This teaching style is used extensively in technology and in other process-based subjects. Where there is a strong emphasis on pupils demonstrating competencies rather than knowledge, the need to develop individual work is increased. Vocational courses are often competency-based. This approach is well suited to able pupils, especially those who, as well as having good ideas, also have the organizational skills to complete tasks effectively. The major disadvantage is the demand on teacher time, making this approach frequently impossible in large classes.

6. Core plus options

This is a pragmatic teaching style which recognizes the need to cover core content but also to make space for responding to the needs of individuals. In this approach it may be that pupils choose options from within a given range, e.g. from the extension tasks, or a free choice, perhaps with an opportunity to 'use and apply' the concepts learnt. One disadvantage here can be in the way the two elements are handled. The core is often very dull, with the interesting work coming later. Also, if able children come to see extension work as additional work, they often dislike it and will slow their workrate to ensure that they only have time to do the core.

Summary

All teaching and learning styles can be used effectively with able pupils. Some styles lend themselves particularly well to certain subjects but can be used in others. All styles have disadvantages for some able pupils and therefore need to be used sensitively.

Creating challenge

At the heart of differentiated extension planning is the creation of challenging tasks. Extension will not be effective if it is:

- more practice of the same ideas,
- the next page or book,
- unrewarded additional work,
- an unplanned, very open activity.

Able pupils are no more hard working than others, and if finishing the core task early leads to 'more work extension' they quickly learn to slow down to fill the time available. Equally, tasks which are very unstructured are not motivating or appealing to most. 'Go and find out all you can about...' is unlikely to lead to the use of extensive research skills and instead may lead to disruption in the library.

In some schools the idea of extension work has been adopted at senior management level but there is little understanding of its nature at classroom level. An assumption is made that all teachers will automatically know how to create extension work and how to monitor its effectiveness. In practice the creation of extension activities is not easy, especially at the start. It is not only about content or what is to be taught, but also about approaches to learning and thinking. It may mean presenting tasks or information in a different way and evolving additional methods of assessing performance. It may mean revisiting existing planning and considering ways in which activities can be slanted to make them more demanding. It may even mean modifying your teaching style.

These types of changes take time and, rather than adding extension to all lessons at once, it is advisable to choose one area for development so that targets can be set and progress monitored. In a secondary school this may be a selected year group which becomes the focus of departmental activity. In a primary school it may be a particular topic or subject. Essential parts of the process are regular opportunities for review and chances to report on success and failures. A collaborative school or departmental approach is particularly helpful here.

When thinking about the nature of extension tasks it is helpful to consider the types of abilities we wish to develop in able pupils. There is broad agreement amongst researchers, although individual interpretations exist as to the importance of particular aspects, that the following abilities are developed through extension tasks:

- independence
- critical thinking
- creative thinking
- problem-solving ability
- reflection
- motivation
- self-knowledge.

An elegant summary of this type of approach came in an OFSTED Inspection Report which was describing an example of good provision: 'Teachers operate securely without untimely intervention and encourage pupils to think, reflect and seek challenges in their tasks'.

Obviously there is no one right way to create extension opportunities but rather a menu of possibilities from which the teacher may choose. Selection may be dependent on the subject in question, on the time available, on the group who will do the task or on the staffing ratio. It is helpful be bear in mind a pupil perspective on this. A selection of able children were questioned on what made learning attractive to them, and certain issues emerged as important to them:

- knowing the long-term framework
- clear short-term goals
  - starting point
  - methods allowed
  - expected outcome
- independence within the task
- elements of choice
- chance to discuss with the teacher
- chance for meaningful evaluation
- teacher articulating what had been learnt and suggesting generalizations.

Twenty possible ways to create challenge in the classroom

The following are some ways to create challenge in the classroom, ranging from the formal to the very informal. They aim to develop the aptitudes outlined in the list of abilities developed through extension tasks given above (see p. 54) and form an *aide-mémoire* for busy teachers. It is not intended in this section to use the list as a basis for exemplification but rather to illustrate a range of extension planning techniques which are appropriate for classroom use. The characteristics in the list pervade in whole, or part, all of the techniques outlined.

1. Plan/do/review

This approach encourages independent thinking and requires the use of both creative and critical thinking. It is used widely in technology but can easily be applied to a variety of other curriculum areas.

With able pupils the first and last stages are particularly important. They should be encouraged to plan systematically and with greater rigour than other children and to give reasons for their planning choices. During the 'doing' section they should be encouraged to be as independent as possible. When I am observing able pupils working in class there is an interesting distinction between those who are encouraged to resolve their own problems and those who are encouraged to seek teacher guidance at the first sign of difficulty. Able pupils need to struggle with difficult ideas because it is often at this point that the real learning occurs. In addition, striving at something in order to succeed is an unfamiliar experience for some able children and failure can be traumatic. They need to learn to work at difficult problems within the secure climate of the classroom. Naturally, some children are better at resolving problems than others. *Learning to Succeed* (The Paul Hamlyn Foundation, 1993) sorts children into two groups: mastery children and helpless children. The first group sees problems and difficulties as a challenge and strives to overcome them. The second group gives up easily, which may be a major factor in children's achievement. In the case of able children the second group are potential able underachievers.

The review aspect of this technique is sometimes of a perfunctory nature in school. To the question, 'How could you improve that next time?', the child may write a low level response, e.g., 'Next time I will write more neatly'. What is needed, especially from the most able, is a high level analytical response. However, they may not be able to achieve this alone and need help in recognizing what they have learnt and how this could be used on future occasions. Teacher time being at a premium in the classroom, it is worth considering the role of paired evaluation and using particular pieces of work for sample evaluations.

Diary of Mrs Pike

February 9th
Todaye hav beene a bussye one. Beth, carters wiffe ande mee hav cooked moste off tomorrows dinner ande supper toe which Parson bee sure toe stoppe etting ande drynking all thee time, butt I doe thynk ther been enuff for I have boyled our biggeste ham ande cooked a sadell off mutten, 3 capons, ande a rounde of spised beefe ande a roste hare wythe his inside filled with herbes ande bitts, then some tartes ande a pritch pudden, some cheese ande butter ande bredd, thys wyth pertaties ande greens ande other trymmings shoulde doe verrie welle, ande there will bee cyder and beere and sherrie wine to drynk, so wee shoule have a goode dinner, ande after I wille sette in thee parlur lyke a ladie and lett Beth putt on thee tay, while I shall worrit in case shee doe brake thee dyshes. Parson Ellis and Thomas doe talke varrie drye, butt I doe have toe sett wyth them Thomas thynking itt bee thee proper thing for mee toe doe, butt later I shall says I muste see that tee bee getting reddy and I muste cutte thee cake, whiche is already done bye Beth, butte Thomas nott noeing thys I can gette away.

I doe hop Mistress Ellis will nott cum shee bein so fussie, butt iff she doe, I shall hav a dish wich will make her want to noe about, I bee bound, for I hav cooked mye mutton thys waye lyke thee Lady Susan didd tell me she doe have itte cooked in her owne kitchen. I doe fill itte whyth a mess made of cutte up union, tyme, and parsley, ande 2 eggs cooked harde, thys bee all chopt upp together whyth sum fatte baccon, then I doe pushe alle intoie thee mutten ande presse inn thee cutt oute piece, ande tye itte harde whyth twyne to hold itt furm, while itte does cooke, when itte bee colde I doe take away thee twyne ande itte doe cutte oute furm.

Iff Mistress Ellis doe cum, I shall give her some butte shalle notte telle her what makes thee fine flavour, shee bein sure to quiss, butt I shall notee saye, soe shee will be madd.

I have no more tyme toe rite nowe, butt goe to bedd and doe hope I will not lye awaike thinken off how much wille bee left off tomorrows joint for next day's dinner.

Figure 3.9 Using difficult text

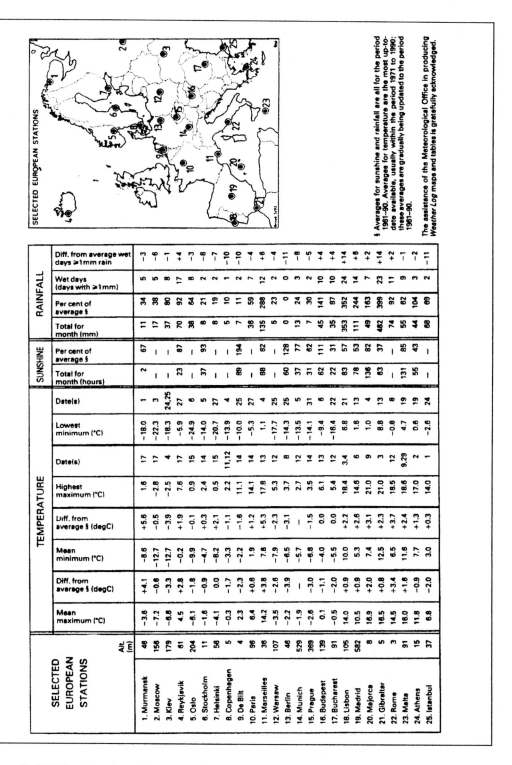

SELECTED EUROPEAN STATIONS

§ Averages for sunshine and rainfall are all for the period 1981–90. Averages for temperature are the most up-to-date available, usually within the period 1971 to 1990; these averages are gradually being updated to the period 1981–90.

The assistance of the Meteorological Office in producing *Weather Log* maps and tables is gratefully acknowledged.

Selected European Stations	Alt. (m)	TEMPERATURE Mean maximum (°C)	Diff. from average § (degC)	Mean minimum (°C)	Diff. from average § (degC)	Highest maximum (°C)	Date(s)	Lowest minimum (°C)	Date(s)	SUNSHINE Total for month (hours)	Per cent of average §	RAINFALL Total for month (mm)	Per cent of average §	Wet days (days with ≥1mm)	Diff. from average wet days ≥1mm rain
1. Murmansk	46	-3.8	+4.1	-8.8	+5.6	1.6	17	-18.0	1	2	67	11	34	5	-3
2. Moscow	156	-7.2	-0.6	-12.7	-0.5	-2.8	17	-22.3	3	–	–	17	38	5	-6
3. Kiev	179	-6.8	-3.3	-12.7	-3.9	-2.5	4	-18.3	24,25	–	–	37	80	8	-1
4. Reykjavik	61	4.5	+2.8	-0.2	+1.9	7.6	17	-5.9	27	23	87	70	92	17	+4
5. Oslo	204	-6.1	-1.8	-9.9	-0.1	0.9	15	-24.9	6	37	93	38	64	8	-3
6. Stockholm	11	-1.6	-0.9	-4.7	+0.3	2.4	14	-14.0	5	–	–	8	21	2	-8
7. Helsinki	56	-4.1	0.0	-8.2	+2.1	0.5	15	-20.7	27	–	–	8	19	2	-7
8. Copenhagen	5	-0.3	-1.7	-3.3	-1.1	2.2	11,12	-13.9	4	89	194	5	10	1	-7
9. De Bilt	4	2.3	-2.3	-2.2	-1.6	11.1	14	-10.0	25	–	–	7	11	2	-10
10. Paris	96	6.4	+0.8	1.9	+1.2	14.1	14	-5.3	27	88	62	36	59	7	-10
11. Marseilles	36	14.2	+3.8	7.8	+5.3	17.8	13	1.1	4	–	–	135	288	12	-4
12. Warsaw	107	-3.5	-2.6	-7.9	-2.3	5.3	12	-17.7	25	60	128	5	23	2	+6
13. Berlin	46	-2.2	-3.9	-6.5	-3.1	3.7	8	-14.3	25	37	77	0	0	0	-4
14. Munich	529	-1.9	—	-5.7	—	2.7	12	-13.5	8	31	62	13	24	3	-11
15. Prague	369	-2.6	-3.0	-6.8	-1.5	3.5	14	-14.1	31	62	111	7	30	2	-8
16. Budapest	139	0.1	-1.1	-4.0	0.0	6.1	13	-9.4	6	22	31	45	141	10	-5
17. Bucharest	91	-0.5	-2.0	-5.5	0.0	5.4	12	-16.4	22	83	57	35	87	10	+4
18. Lisbon	105	14.0	+0.9	10.0	+2.2	18.4	3,4	6.8	21	78	53	353	352	24	+4
19. Madrid	582	10.5	+0.9	5.3	+2.6	14.5	6	1.8	13	136	82	111	244	14	+14
20. Majorca	8	16.9	+2.0	7.4	+3.1	21.0	9	1.0	4	63	37	49	163	7	+8
21. Gibraltar	5	16.5	+0.8	12.5	+2.3	21.0	3	8.8	13	–	–	482	399	23	+14
22. Rome	3	14.5	+3.4	6.5	+3.7	18.5	12	-0.8	8	131	85	74	92	11	+2
23. Malta	91	16.0	+1.6	11.6	+2.4	18.6	9,29	4.7	19	55	43	55	62	9	-1
24. Athens	15	11.8	-0.9	7.7	+1.3	17.0	2	0.6	19	–	–	44	104	3	-2
25. Istanbul	37	6.8	-2.0	3.0	+0.3	14.0	1	-2.6	24	–	–	88	69	2	-11

Figure 3.10 Weather log: January 1996

2. Working from difficult text

This immediately increases the level of difficulty. Able pupils can work on the same topic or even activity as other children, but make use of a more adult or sophisticated text. Extension tasks can be set using information extracted from the text. The advantages of using more complex text are twofold. A more complex text is likely to have more detailed information and, as it was written for an older age group, may address more complex issues, rather like reading an article in a broadsheet rather than a tabloid newspaper. Of course, what constitutes a 'difficult text' varies according to the age and the ability of the group.

History lends itself easily to the use of first-hand sources. The text in Figure 3.9 forms part of a project on a Victorian village (Adams *et al.*, 1987). This piece encourages children to write in the style of the diary author and to complete the diary entry for the day of the visit. The task could be done by able pupils, but the outcome will have interest and relevance for the whole class.

Fiction can also be used in this way. Pupils can be encouraged to read more challenging texts to support work done on a class text. They may look at another book in the same genre or in which similar plot construction is used. They may look at a pre-twentieth century text or a less accessible twentieth century one.

Perhaps the most difficult text to access is official text, be it in the form of data or local government papers. The example in Figure 3.10 is a weather log (Royal Meteorological Society, 1996). It is typical of the sort of resource material which is readily available to schools and which can easily be used to extend the normal classroom exploration of weather into something more challenging.

3. Using a range of text or information

This offers instant opportunities for a range of comparative work. With multimedia information available it is possible to make use of books and CD-ROMs as well as pictures and videos. Indeed information is so freely available that the tasks set will probably focus on extracting key information or specific data rather than finding out as much as possible.

Able pupils should be helped to develop the study skills to enable them to sift through a wide variety of material to reach conclusions. Extension tasks may be used to develop such study skills. Setting this type of task has both management and resource implications for schools. Effective comparisons cannot be made without appropriate resource materials and making use of them may involve working in the library or other spaces outside the classroom.

Example

This example of using a variety of text is fiction-based and comes from Uffington CE Primary School, a rural primary school. The Year 3/4 class was working on John Burningham's Mr Gumpy books. All the class looked at Mr Gumpy's Motor Car and Mr Gumpy's Outing and compared the two books with a view to writing their own Mr Gumpy book. Everyone recognized the formula for the stories and incorporated it into their books. The most able also modelled the language usage. Two very able children then looked at a variety of other John Burningham books to see if they could find common threads in his work. This worked very well because John

Burningham has an unusual way of linking pictures and text and, although it is more pronounced in some books than others, it is a common feature of all his books, which the two most able pupils could discover.

4. Recording in an unusual way

The vast majority of the work children do in school is still recorded in a written format. There are a variety of reasons for this, ranging from ease of storage and assessment through to sheer habit. When planning extension work, it is worth thinking about other forms of recording, as writing is disliked by many children; as has been mentioned previously, extension work which is done in addition to core work needs to be motivating and interesting or pupils will resent doing it.

Another point worth mentioning is the grouping of able pupils who do not find writing easy. If all extension work requires a written outcome then they will be unable to complete it satisfactorily. Extension work should aim to develop thinking and be less concerned with how that thinking is conveyed.

Finally, it is important that extension work does not become dislocated from other class activity and one way to avoid this is to make use of recording techniques which will involve, be of interest to or supplement the work of others. Examples include presentations using OHP, tape recordings and memos or the creation of models.

Example

In a topic on the Tudors, the extension group considered the length of reign of each of the Tudor monarchs and recorded this in a bar chart for use by the rest of the class. This led to a class discussion focusing on the major events in the reign of each monarch and the relationship between the number of events and the length of reign.

5. Role play

This is simply an easy way to require children to act in a different way or respond to information they would not usually meet. The Year 7 Civil War history project in a school which had Civil War connections used first-hand sources and then required pupils to write a diary for a person of the period. This is both more interesting and more challenging than a series of lessons on the Civil War. Able pupils will research to make their diary authentic and can be encouraged to make use of the local public records office.

The example in Figure 3.11 is a Year 6 child writing about an historical event from a variety of viewpoints.

6. Problem-solving and enquiry tasks

Most problem-solving activities require children to engage in higher level thinking. It is a helpful short-cut in extension planning to consider whether the tasks to cover the content or concepts required could be set in such a way as to involve enquiry. Even the most straightforward work can be made more interesting and challenging by presentation through enquiry.

Diary of Petra Carrson
14th March 1595

Rumour has it that the reivers are coming soon! I go all shivery as I write the words. A neighbouring farmer galloped over to tell us this morning. When mother heard, she covered her face with her hands and ran from the table, crying. I started to shake and Papa held me on his lap like he did when I was little. When I had eventually calmed down, he told me to fetch some milk from the dairy, I did but when I was walking back I heard a distressed servant shouting, "They'll be heere tomorra neet!" and gasps from the listeners. As I heard this my knees collapsed beneath me, I heard the thud as my head hit the floor and everything went black.

A School History Book

During the years 1500 to 1650, terrible robbing gangs roamed the border country between England and Scotland. They were called Reivers. They attacked or reived houses and stole food, clothes and animals. Several stories exist today about their frightening activities. One well-known raid was when the Carrson house was attacked. The reivers set the Carrson house on fire and stole everything of value. Then, when grandfather Armstrong attempted to stop them, he was shot. The rest of the family then escaped to Tullie House in Carlisle where they lived for six months, before moving to and settling in Manchester. A museum can be found in Carlisle today in Mr James Tullie's name. If you are ever in the area, you may wish to visit it, to discover more about these events.

Tullie House
Carlisle
Cumberland

31st March 1595

My dearest Margaret

I write to you in deepest sorrow. As you will gather from the address, we are lodging at Tullie House, the reason being that not long ago the reivers (I shudder to write this) destroyed our house by fire. Before they came (we heard news of their coming) we managed to pack a few necessities and flee.

But then the Reivers arrived. They sang a victory song and set our great house and the surrounding buildings alight with blazing torches. We were terrified and paralysed by their power.

Figure 3.11 'The Rievers: a story' Bryony Dean, aged 11

Poor Papa. He was killed in the most cowardly way, when he staggered out of the burning house. He threatened the Reivers with swords, but they shot him with muskets. I sobbed and shrieked over Papa and covered myself with his blood when I sat him up and hugged him. I placed his granddaughter, Clara, in his arms and shouted curses at the Reivers. Then I escaped into the dark night with Peter and the children.

The rest of us struggled on, through bad weather, especially very fierce storms. The children were constantly frightened and Clara contracted fever, poor thing. She nearly died of choking, as we cowered in a hedge. After two weeks of struggle, we had entered the town of Carlisle and were taken in by an old friend, a kind man by the name of Mr James Tullie. We are now living in his happy house. It is our intention to escape the border area.

Yours dearly
Anne

THE DAILY BORDER
Carrson Home Destroyed in Raid

Late on the night of 13th March, the Carson house was attacked by Reivers. Apparently, according to the mother, Mrs Anne Carrson, they approached on horseback at the dead of night.

The grandfather, Osbert Armstrong, was shot dead when trying to halt the evil deeds of the attacking reivers. The reivers stole horses, cattle, food, money and jewellery. They burnt the house to the ground and then left at approximately two o'clock.

The rest of the family are currently lodging at Mr James Tullie's house in Carlisle, to which they escaped on that fearful night. No one else was hurt, but Anne Carson's two year old daughter, Clara, has a severe fever. The whole family are suffering from severe shock.

The Carrson and Armstrong families are respected ones in this area, especially Osbert Armstrong who lived in his house for eighty four years. The family was joined to the Carrsons when Peter Carrson married Anne Armstrong, as reported in this journal 14 years ago. The house was an extensive one, richly appointed, with many servants, but it has suffered cruelly from the fire deliberately caused by the murderous intruders. Sadly, it now stands ruined and derelict. Since the disaster the family have been trying to settle down to normal family life in another part of England.

Diary of Petra Carrson
10th October 1595

I am writing this dairy entry in the nursery that I share with Clara in our new house in Manchester. On 21st September, we left Tullie House and started our journey to the new house that Papa has bought. Glory be! Tonight I can go to bed and feel secure in the knowledge that I can sleep until the morning sun shines on my face. Today I went to fetch milk. I spent the whole journey enjoying the safety of the town. Tomorrow I shall get out of bed and rush outside and greet the morning and my new life that awaits me.

Figure 3.11 Continued

Example

A maths group had been learning subtraction with units, tens and hundreds. The teacher was aware that the group now had a thorough understanding of the skills involved but did not want them to start a new area of work until the following week when she could introduce the new area to everyone with a whole-class lesson. So, she gave the group a page of subtraction sums and asked them to do only the questions on the page where the last two digits of the answer were even or the answer was divisible by 3. Of course in order to decide whether they needed to do the sum the children had to either work out each of the answers or devise a strategy for determining whether the sums fell into the required categories.

Problem solving has become very popular in primary schools. Unfortunately, children are often simply given the problem and asked to investigate it without clear guidance on possible routes forward. This leads to a good deal of wasted time and children becoming frustrated. Children need to be taught problem-solving techniques which enable them to decide how to begin to address the problem and how to assess progress. Robert Fisher covers this well in his book *Teaching Children to Think* (1990). Fisher identifies some factors which influence the problem-solving process (see Figure 3.12). These demonstrate why able pupils are, generally, such effective problem solvers. They have high cognitive ability and may also have significant experience. However, the attitude factors are not a constant feature with able pupils. Some able pupils have a low tolerance of ambiguity or may lack confidence. These able pupils often dislike

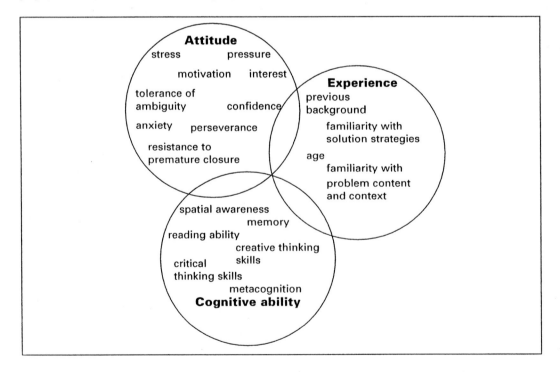

Figure 3.12 Some factors in the problem solving process

problem solving, especially if it is very open-ended and unstructured. Such children can often be helped to become more efficient problem solvers by structuring the task in such a way as to require them to undertake certain key investigations before proceeding more generally.

Some of the most interesting problems at both primary and secondary level concern the solving of real problems. These have the advantage of real purpose and are therefore particularly motivating. They also help pupils engage with school, which is a significant issue for those able youngsters who drift off into their own world when the classroom activity seems uninteresting.

Example 1

A pair of good mathematicians in Year 2 were given a problem related to car parking. The school was to have a celebration to open a new set of classrooms. This was an important event for the school and a large number of guests were expected. The headteacher explained that they needed to make the most effective use possible of the playground for car parking. Could his Year 2 pair make any suggestions? They set about the task in a systematic manner, measuring the largest car they could find and then deciding on a scale for a scale drawing. They asked for guidance on two issues before they could draw up the plan: whether everyone would be leaving at the same time or whether they needed to leave space for cars to exit on demand; and whether the head thought that drivers would mind sliding over to the passenger side to get out, if their car was placed next to a wall! These queries epitomize the approach of able pupils. The first is thoughtful and reflective, the second is thoughtful but also very typical of a 7-year-old. Able pupils may be intellectually able, but they are still children and should be allowed a childhood.

In a school it is tempting to give all such problems to the oldest children but school policy should ensure a fair distribution.

Example 2

Sonning Common Primary had identified a problem related to children who join the school from other schools. How could they be helped to settle more quickly? One idea was a handbook for children which would be issued to them when their parents received the school prospectus and would contain useful information for them. A group of Year 4s drew up the handbook and produced it. It contained a combination of fact and interruption; here is a quote from it:

> Table Tennis. If you get table tennis bats and a ball from the football shed you do not hit people with the bats. Do not do anything except table-tennis with the balls because they are not very strong. There are other things to borrow at playtime and the monitors give them out and collect them.

Example 3

An extension group of Years 7, 8 and 9 solved a problem for Warwick Tourist Office. They wanted a trail around Warwick for visually impaired visitors. The group devised the trail using head phones and tape, as part of a weekend school residential for able pupils.

7. Choice in how to handle content

Creating opportunities for choice has many benefits. It increases motivation and may encourage pupils to work longer and harder on a task. It is particularly useful with the sort of able pupil who stubbornly refuses to do anything for which she or he cannot see a purpose, and helps to engage the daydreamer.

From a teaching point of view it is part of the strategy for able pupil provision. If we are encouraging pupils to reflect and seek challenges in their tasks, they are likely, when given the opportunity to choose, to select a difficult and challenging route. This is a kind a differentiation through choice. Talking to many able pupils, especially in secondary schools, they mention ways in which they would have liked to explore the concept or content. Their ideas are often less conventional than the teacher might have planned for extension but equally valuable and challenging. It is not always possible to give choice but where it is possible it should be encouraged.

A note of caution here regarding those able pupils who suffer low self-esteem and are unlikely to judge themselves capable of a difficult option. It is sometimes necessary for the teacher to guide the choices of this kind of able pupil and make it clear that in their view the child is more than capable of tackling the task.

8. Decision making

Once again this is a fast and easy way to ensure that able pupils are required to think. For some able pupils making decisions is quite a problem and is a skill which needs to be developed. For others it is an area of greater expertise and they will give their opinions confidently and with great clarity.

Sometimes a task can be set at a more difficult level simply by asking pupils to make decisions about what should be included and what should be left out. In the following example a problem-solving activity has been extended by adding a decision-making element.

Example

This primary school had a problem with parking. When the supermarket next door became crowded, the cars were parked across the school drive causing disruption and danger. The extension group surveyed parents and local residents to see if they could find a solution. They wanted to tell the supermarket manager everything that they had found out, but the teacher insisted on half a page of A4 maximum as the manager was a busy man. This constraint completely changed the task. The group had to decide what was important enough to go in – a much more difficult task than just reporting everything.

Able children often have to learn decision-making skills earlier than other children. For many children in the primary school written work often amounts to 'writing everything you know about...'. Able pupils have to decide which parts of their extensive knowledge to discard. One Year 6 child, explaining to me why he couldn't start on his piece of work about the evacuation of Dunkirk observed, 'There is so much you could say about this and I know she only wants about a page. Which bits do you think she wants?'

9. No correct answer

This is linked to decision making and requires pupils to make selections and justify their choice. For some able pupils this is not easy. They like a clear set of instructions and the corresponding set of ticks for right answers. This kind of able pupil, at whatever age, will seek reassurance on a regular basis. They may ask questions such as, 'Is this the real answer?', as if the teacher already has an answer but is unwilling to share it. This kind of pupil needs to be encouraged to take risks.

For the majority of able pupils, open-ended tasks which do not have a set answer are a joy. They will explore aspects the teacher had not thought of and feel real satisfaction in finding a justifiable answer. Such tasks usually require pupils to use their critical thinking skills as well as to make use of a wide variety of information.

10. Give the answer, they set the question

This is a form of differentiation by outcome which can be used with all ages. From the teaching perspective it enables the whole class or group to work on the same task but with differing outcomes. As always with differentiation by outcome, there is a need for the teacher to have considered possible learning outcomes so as to support or facilitate.

It is sometimes interesting to use this technique as a final aspect of a piece of work. After the pupils have worked through a task, asking them to create a similar task for others again makes use of higher level thinking, in this case synthesis. A simple example of this would be a crossword: first to complete one and then to create one for others – a more difficult task.

11. Using one text or artefact

When planning extension work it is often assumed that more resources will be needed and that pupils will explore additional aspects which enhance existing classroom provision. This is, of course, one form of extension planning but an equally effective form works in reverse. By limiting the use of material it forces pupils to consider the material in more depth and can allow pupils to develop a much greater understanding. The infant department of a Bristol school, for example, used *The Snowman*, by Raymond Briggs, as the basis of a month's work. Good quality books or artefacts are needed to support this type of extension planning, but many of both are freely available.

12. Allowing pupils to do the planning

Many teachers when talking about differentiation complain about the amount of time that it takes to plan for a range of outcomes. In reality this planning is not always as arduous as is sometimes suggested in that often only a minor adjustment in the slant of the task is required to make it more challenging. One way in which such planning can be made easier, and at the same time encouraging greater pupil involvement, is by letting pupils do their own planning, sharing the basic planning with the group and then asking for suggestions for possible alternatives. Often able pupils will think up ingenious ideas which may not have occurred to the teacher. When talking to able children they often give ideas for ways in which the lesson they have just experienced could have been improved. Interestingly, their ideas usually involve more difficult tasks than the ones set by the teacher. If we are keen to encourage children to think, then establishing a climate where it is possible to negotiate an adaptation to the set class task is one way to facilitate this.

13. Time-restricted activities

Another way to create challenge is to restrict the amount of time available to accomplish the task. What may be a reasonably straightforward task can become much more difficult if limited time is available. Pupils may need to make decisions regarding what is possible rather than what is desirable and subsequently resolve a series of compromises. This sort of approach can lead to the production of better work from some able children and is especially effective with disenchanted boys.

Example

The class had to work on a class newspaper, with each group taking charge of one section of the paper. The paper was to go to press at lunchtime and any incomplete work would leave blank spaces in the layout. The most able group was making excellent progress and would probably have finished the task before the deadline. However, 30 minutes before lunch the teacher broke a major new story – accident on local bypass. The group had 30 minutes to write up the story and reschedule the front page.

This kind of task cannot be used all the time but has a useful place as part of the extension menu. The teacher here was covering journalistic writing; this could easily have been covered in a less imaginative way, but with less impressive results.

14. Developing metacognition

Robert Fisher (1990) describes metacognitive knowledge as knowing how you know things and the process by which you think. Metacognitive skills help us to acquire control of our thinking. In the past 20 years this focus on metacognition has gained a significant following in a number of different educational arenas. Recognizing one's own thinking processes and, through that, developing or enhancing thinking has influenced the work of educators from nursery school to management training. This approach has considerable advantages in helping able pupils to become more independent in their learning and gaining better self-knowledge. Of all children they are the ones who can make the most use of metacognitive information and therefore are likely to benefit from exposure to it.

Researchers like Reuven Feuerstein (1980) believe that children fail because they do not have the appropriate tools for learning and that they can be taught such skills in order to facilitate success. Metacognitive work may well be a case of extension for all rather than for a nominated group, since all pupils can benefit from it.

Thinking skills can be taught in two ways: through intellectual games and through the curriculum. The first approach, usually called 'instrumental enrichment', is taught as a separate subject or activity. Children are introduced to the tools through activities which require no background knowledge. The Somerset Thinking Skills Course by Blagg *et al.* (1988) is an example of this approach. The second method is by drawing children's attention to their thinking processes as part of general classroom activity, teaching them to see themselves as learners and to recognize their strengths and weaknesses. Instrumental enrichment has sometimes been criticized because researchers have been unable to find evidence of children transferring their thinking skills work into their ordinary learning.

The second approach negates the need for this bridging by setting the tasks within the subject context. One well reported example of this is the CASE (Cognitive Accelerated Science Education) work of Shayer and Adey (1981) which is aimed at science and maths teaching in middle secondary level. Robert Fisher (1987) has also developed this approach for use in primary schools.

When planning extension activities it is possible to make a conscious effort to develop metacognitive skills, encouraging pupils to think about the thinking processes which they are using as well as the task to be undertaken.

15. Bloom's higher order thinking

If pressed to identify an approach to extension planning which is particularly useful, this would be my choice. It has a clear structure to enable planning and is easily adapted to a wide variety of subject areas. I have used this approach extensively with both primary and secondary schools in inservice work and found it an effective way to extend existing classroom planning. The approach was first developed by Bloom (1956) and has been adapted for use in general classroom planning. The approach identifies the characteristics of high and low level thinking and can be used to focus on ways in which more high level tasks can be included. The diagram in Figure 3.13 shows the levels as building blocks.

Kerry (1984) found that in first-year secondary classrooms, 85 per cent of the tasks observed could be described as low level and 15 per cent as high level. No research exists to indicate the proportion at the present time, but anecdotal evidence would suggest a continuing heavy emphasis on the lower levels. A focus on extending classroom planning to include the higher levels can lead to extension tasks for a group of the most able or sometimes an increase in cognitive demand for the whole class. What is particularly interesting about this approach is that, while it may be quite difficult to relate to immediately, once a teacher has attempted to plan this way on one or two sample modules it becomes a very natural way of planning and enters the teachers' planning repertoire on a permanent basis.

Oxfordshire teachers have illustrated the versatility of this approach by producing examples of the ways in which they have extended their existing classroom planning using this technique. An interesting by-product of this work was an increased understanding of the way in which National Curriculum Attainment Target 1 in maths and science relates to other areas of those subjects. Figures 3.14 to 3.18 illustrate a variety of ideas based on Bloom.

68

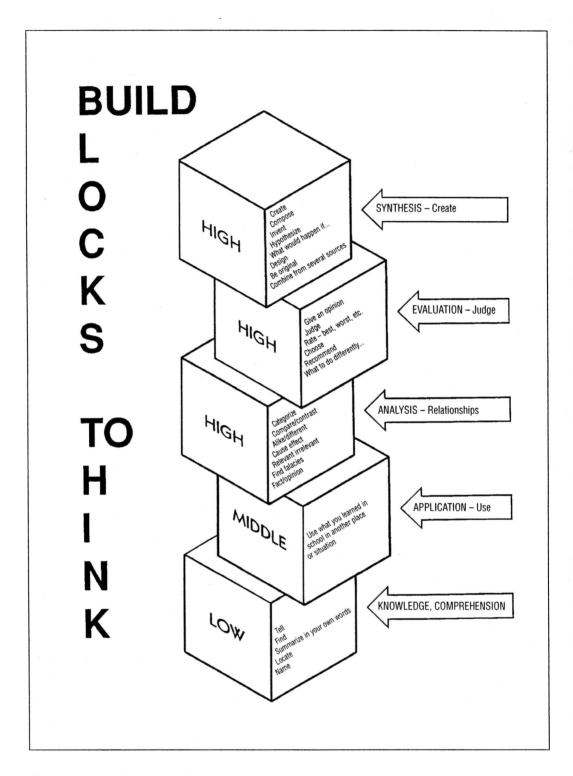

BUILD

L
O
C
K
S

TO

T
H
I
N
K

HIGH

Create
Compose
Invent
Hypothesize
What would happen if...
Design
Be original
Combine from several sources

SYNTHESIS – Create

HIGH

Give an opinion
Judge
Rate – best, worst, etc.
Choose
Recommend
What to do differently...

EVALUATION – Judge

HIGH

Categorize
Compare/contrast
Alike/different
Cause effect
Relevant irrelevant
Find falacies
Fact/opinion

ANALYSIS – Relationships

MIDDLE

Use what you learned in
school in another place
or situation

APPLICATION – Use

LOW

Tell
Find
Summarize in your own words
Locate
Name

KNOWLEDGE, COMPREHENSION

Figure 3.13 Bloom's building blocks

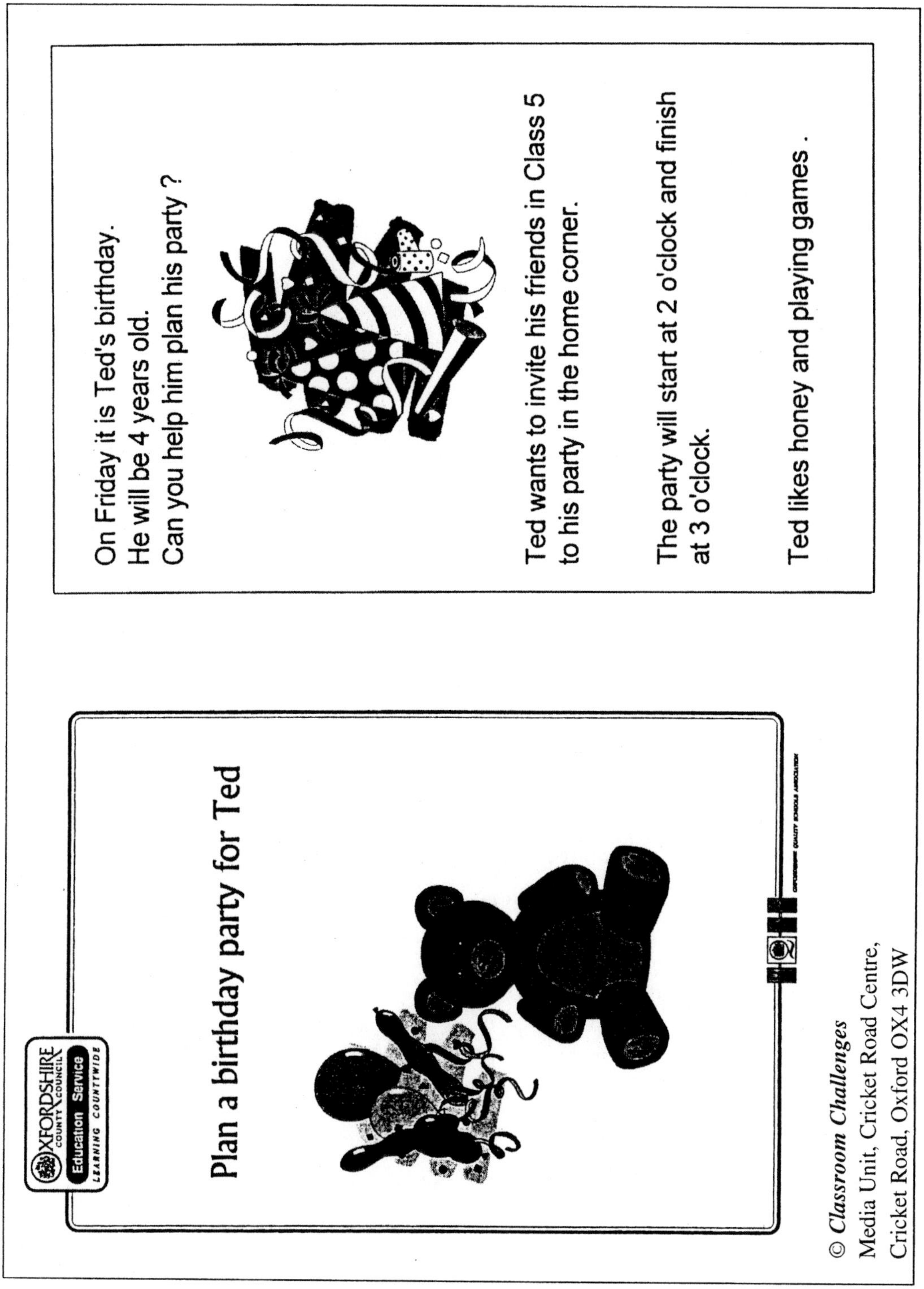
OXFORDSHIRE COUNTY COUNCIL
Education Service
LEARNING COUNTYWIDE
Plan a birthday party for Ted
© *Classroom Challenges*
Media Unit, Cricket Road Centre,
Cricket Road, Oxford OX4 3DW
On Friday it is Ted's birthday.
He will be 4 years old.
Can you help him plan his party ?
Ted wants to invite his friends in Class 5 to his party in the home corner.
The party will start at 2 o'clock and finish at 3 o'clock.
Ted likes honey and playing games .

Figures 3.14 Plan a birthday party for Ted

Can you .....

1. Design the invitation

2. Think of games you will play

3. Make up a new party game

4. Make a plan of when you will play the games and have tea

5. Make a list of the food for the party

6. Make pretend plates of the food

7. What decorations do you need to make ?

8. Get everything ready

CONGRATULATIONS
you have finished !

How did the party go ?

Figures 3.14 Continued

OXFORDSHIRE COUNTY COUNCIL
Education Service
LEARNING COUNTYWIDE
A RIVER CROSSING
Locate a local river on a map
Look at the land use around the river: buildings, fields, paths, roads etc.
Decide on two points along the course which are interesting (they have crossing points such as fords or bridges)
Visit the two points
Measure the depth and width of the river, draw a cross-section
Where is the water shallow ?
Where is the water deepest ?
Where is the flow fastest ?

Figures 3.15 The river crossing

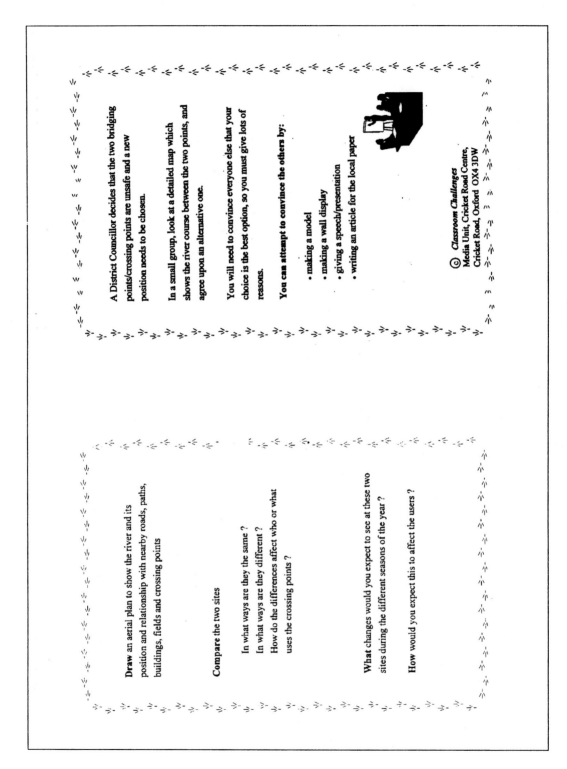

Draw an aerial plan to show the river and its position and relationship with nearby roads, paths, buildings, fields and crossing points

Compare the two sites

In what ways are they the same ?
In what ways are they different ?
How do the differences affect who or what uses the crossing points ?

What changes would you expect to see at these two sites during the different seasons of the year ?

How would you expect this to affect the users ?

A District Councillor decides that the two bridging points/crossing points are unsafe and a new position needs to be chosen.

In a small group, look at a detailed map which shows the river course between the two points, and agree upon an alternative one.

You will need to convince everyone else that your choice is the best option, so you must give lots of reasons.

You can attempt to convince the others by:

- making a model
- making a wall display
- giving a speech/presentation
- writing an article for the local paper

© *Classroom Challenges*
Media Unit, Cricket Road Centre,
Cricket Road, Oxford OX4 3DW

Figures 3.15 Continued

73

Figures 3.16 The lottery

74

Record Sheet

My guess which number(s)	Actual number(s)	Correct	Wrong

© *Classroom Challenges*
Media Unit, Cricket Road Centre,
Cricket Road, Oxford OX4 3DW

Practical Work

Is there much of a real chance of winning such a lot of money ?

Try this .....

Throw a dice.
Try to PREDICT the actual number which will come up.
How often were you right ?

Try predicting with two, then three dice.
Do you get better at predicting the numbers ?
Use the record sheet overleaf to record how often you guessed which was the correct numbers (s)

Figures 3.16 Continued

75

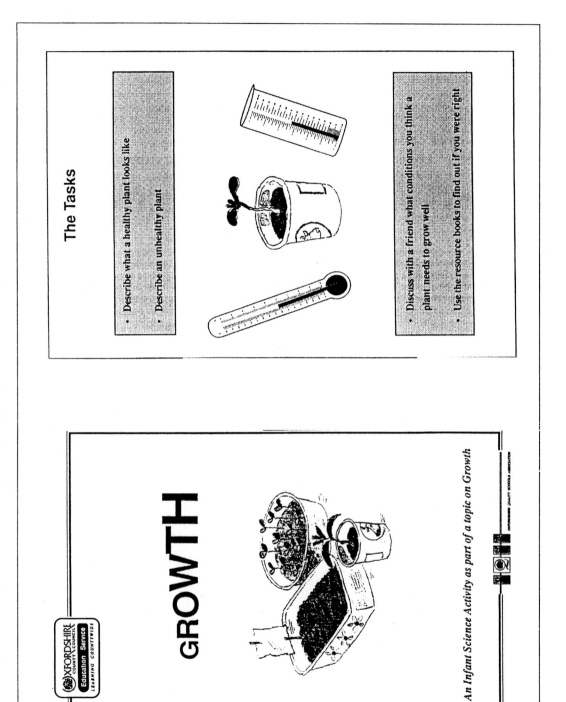

Figures 3.17 Growth

76

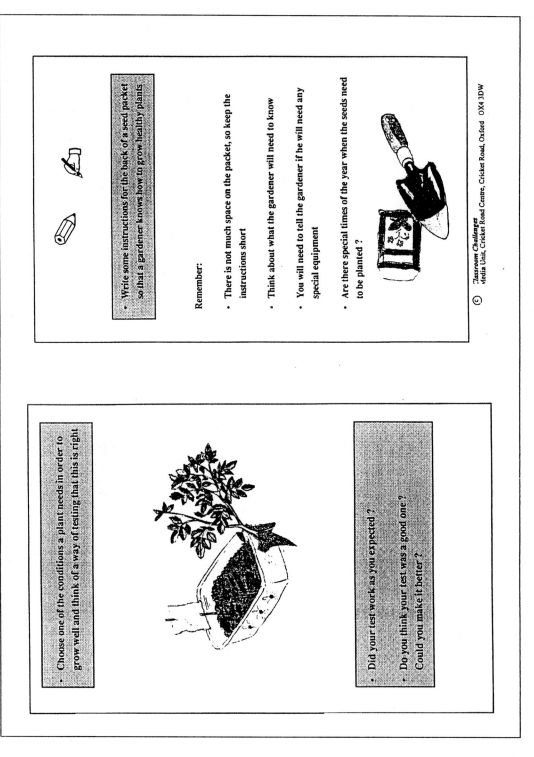

- Write some instructions for the back of a seed packet so that a gardener knows how to grow healthy plants

Remember:

- There is not much space on the packet, so keep the instructions short

- Think about what the gardener will need to know

- You will need to tell the gardener if he will need any special equipment

- Are there special times of the year when the seeds need to be planted?

- Choose one of the conditions a plant needs in order to grow well and think of a way of testing that this is right

- Did your test work as you expected?

- Do you think your test was a good one? Could you make it better?

Figures 3.17 Continued

When we read stories or information we are given that particular writer's point of view. The same information could be presented quite differently by another writer who has an alternative viewpoint. This is clearly shown in the traditional story of "The 3 Little Pigs" and in Jon Scieszka's version "The True Story of the 3 Little Pigs".
Read both.

Discuss with your partner/group what you think about both stories.
Can you separate the facts from the interpretation of the facts? Write 2 separate lists under these headings:

Facts   Interpretation of facts

"A storm in a pig's house"

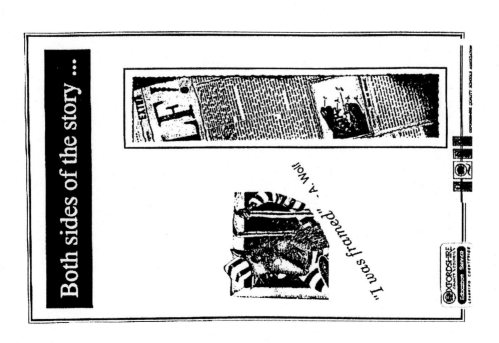

Figures 3.18 Both sides of the story

THE DAILY PIG

"*Misunderstood* — *not* a *murderer*"
... declares wolf in pig scandal.

"*Just Desserts !* "

© *Classroom Challenges*
Media Unit, Cricket Road Centre,
Cricket Road, Oxford   OX4 3DW

You now have to construct a defence of one of those points of view. Work out your own title (a few have been suggested around these pages to help you) and then write your defence, clearly giving your reasons.   You must make it convincing !!!

Read your account to the rest of your group/class - does it convince them? Perhaps they could take a vote on it.

What other stories can you think of that you might look at from both sides of the story? Write some headlines of titles for these stories.

"*They went down squealing*"
... as little pig tells of horror death of his 2 brothers.

Figures 3.18 Continued

16. Study skills, using DARTS

Many useful educational ideas can be successfully adapted for use with able pupils. In the case of learning approaches like DARTS (Directed Activities Related to Text) the major adaptation is in the text used and in the degree of teacher support given. DARTS was created to assist pupils who were having difficulty in accessing text. It therefore works very well with able pupils as a means of accessing very dense or complex text. This allows the teacher to make use of a text which might at first seem inappropriately difficult; for example, a primary teacher working on the Victorians may be able to make use of a section from Oliver Twist. Whilst some work with DARTS may be as a class-based lesson and teacher-led, it is also possible to encourage able pupils to adopt it as part of their general approach to learning. In this instance they apply a DARTS technique whenever they meet a text which proves difficult.

A summary of the DARTS approach (for which I am grateful to my colleague Penny Hollander) is as follows:

DARTS was devised by Lunzer *et al.* (1984) to enable students to 'get into' text. Each activity requires the student to work on the text in some way. It has been found more effective when the students worked in pairs or small groups than when left to tackle text on their own.

The DARTS approach is roughly divided into two types. When the student is required to work directly upon texts that appeared either in textbooks or in work sheets they are called ANALYSIS DARTS. When the student is presented with a modified text, i.e. when the teacher has deleted words or information, it is called RECONSTRUCTION DARTS. Both types encourage pupils to think and reflect on the text.

Analysis DARTS

Underlining. Pupils are asked to underline key words in the text in response to teacher questions.

Labelling. Pupils are asked to classify or label segments of the text.

Constructing diagrams. Using information given in the text, pupils display this in diagrams or graphs.

Tabular representations. Pupils construct tables using the text.

Questions. Pupils read the text and then set questions based on it.

Summarising. Pupils summarise using any of the techniques outlined above.

Reconstruction DARTS

Text Completion. The pupils are given text in which the teacher has deliberately omitted or deleted words or phases. The students have to reconstruct the gaps. Pupils tend to read and think through the passages with much more care than they normally would. This can be done in a number of ways:

- regular deletions every 8, 9 or 10 words,
- specific deletions, e.g. adjectives,
- sentence deletion.

Diagram or table completion. Using the text for guidance the pupils have to insert missing information.

Sequencing. Pupils are presented with scrambled text which has to re-ordered in order to make sense of the text.

Prediction. Students are given the text in sequence and asked to predict what would happen next.

Figure 3.19 shows an example of Hollander using DARTS activities as part of work on World War II.

17. Introducing technical language

The early introduction of technical language allows able pupils to be more rigorous in explaining their ideas. Without the appropriate technical language a child is often unable to explain their thinking processes, so making it more difficult for the teacher to recognize both their current level of thinking and also what Vygotsky (1978) calls their 'zone of proximal development' (ZPD).

Sometimes in educational circles there has been a reluctance to make use of technical language for fear that it may alienate some children. At its worst this has led to a simplification of the reading content of all worksheets and in some cases the simplification of language in the school prospectus. This approach can be very patronizing. Whilst there is no justification for an unnecessarily complex style, this does not mean the elimination of appropriate technical language. If a child is attempting to generalize in maths, knowing that the term for such a process is generalization allows him or her to explain what he or she is attempting to do. It may even be that introducing the technical language actually facilities an understanding of the process.

18. Modelling experts

One effective way of creating challenge is to introduce into the classroom an expert with skills which pupils may wish to emulate. This has a number of advantages. Generally, experts are very good at explaining their subject because they have thought about it deeply and understand it thoroughly. In the classroom context they often talk with great enthusiasm and capture the interest of pupils.

For the most able pupils there are additional advantages linked to that thorough understanding. Pupils are able to ask questions at any level, no matter how difficult, and expect a considered response. Indeed experts are often highly gratified when a pupil asks a really insightful question, whereas a teacher may be irritated by such a diversion from the lesson's planned route. Experts may be working with the class on a particular skill, e.g. poetry or narrative writing; this skill may be developed in greater depth using an expert and therefore may be particularly relevant for the most able.

An additional bonus in using experts lies in their ability to raise the expectations of pupils. Having met a real author, becoming one may seem more attainable. Equally the scientist whose work appears in major scientific journals may seem more human when he explains his love of cricket or football. It should be noted here that experts do not always have to come from beyond the school community. Many parents have much to offer, as do many staff.

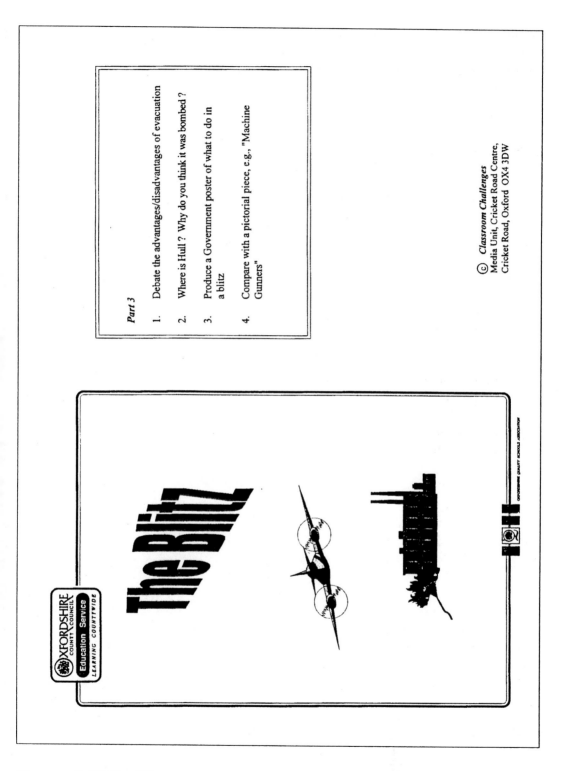

Figures 3.19 The Blitz

Account of the blitz by a Hull secondary school girl, summer 1941

Since August 1940 Hull has been one of the worst badly blitzed areas in England, the worst blitzes being during May, June, July when the main shops of Hull such as Hammonds, the Coop and Thornton-Varley's, were burned.

The raid that affected me most was the one on Saturday, February 22nd, 1941. That night I was in the house of my friend Mary, and at about 8.30 the sirens sounded.

At nine o'clock we began to think the all-clear would be heard soon when, suddenly, all the guns on earth seemed to fire at once, and the Luftwaffe machines droned overhead.

About 10 minutes later we breathed a sigh of relief. The Jerries had passed over without dropping any bombs - or so we thought.

Mary's mother said we had better go down into the shelter while we had a chance.

Just as we were beginning to think the Germans had forgotten about us, the guns started booming, and, once again, we could hear the drone of enemy aircraft overhead.

Suddenly, there was a terrific crash and the shelter door blew in and hit Mary's mother on the leg, not causing any serious injury, however.

We found it impossible to remain in the shelter, because of smoke and dust, so we climbed out and ran into the street. The scene at the other end of Rowlston Grove was one of devastation and ruin. There were women, children and wardens running to and fro carrying sandbags and telling everyone to keep calm.

The fire engine came clanging down the street to put out a fiercely burning fire which a burst gas-pipe and someone's kitchen fire had caused. When we asked a policeman what had happened he told us a land mine had dropped.

A warden came to us and asked our names and addresses as they wanted to check on people who were missing.

We then went to see how Mary's house had suffered. Though it was still standing, it was impossible to live in again.

At 10.30 p.m. the all-clear was sounded, and Mary came with me to our house to see how it had fared.

We found it in a worse condition and my mother, who had been at my aunt's house, was just about to come for me.

As it was impossible for me to do anything then, I went to stay the night in my sister-in-law's house and Mary went to her grandmother's.

We spent the next morning excavating what was left of our furniture and clothing. I spent ten minutes trying to find my gym tunic, which had been hung in front of my wardrobe, and my brother asked me if a rather dirty looking object on the top of a wireless pole was it. So I shook the pole and eventually down came the gym slip.

Needless to say, I did not wear it again until it had been cleaned.

During the latter part of February and the whole of March I stayed at my sister-in-law's house until we got a new home in Portobello Street.

Part 1

1. Draw a scene before and after the raid

2. Produce a timetable of events and add your own

3. Write a list of the characters involved

4. Draw a plan of where people were at the time of the blitz

5. Write a newspaper report

* * * * * * *

Part 2

1. Write either a description of or an interview about a missing child in the blitz

2. What might a blind person hear during a blitz

3. List five favourite objects to take into a shelter

Figure 3.19 Continued

Some schools use experts not just because of their impact on pupils but also as a means of staff development. Staff can model from experts, just as pupils can, and the use of an expert with the class can increase the teacher's own understanding of that particular aspect of the subject.

19. Philosophy

The use of philosophy in the classroom is another way to encourage children to think critically. Perhaps the most well known exponent of this approach is Matthew Lipman (Lipman *et al.*, 1980) but there is now a wide range of educationalists who are interested in this field and even an Institute for the Advancement of Philosophy in Children at Montclair State College in New Jersey. Karen Murris has developed the idea of teaching philosophy using picture books. This is an interesting technique which can be used with a wide variety of age groups. In her book *Philosophy with Picture Books* (1992) she provides a structured approach to the development of philosophical thought. She gives clear guidance on possible questions and on the art of directing philosophical discussion, as well as using examples from a variety of well known picture books. She describes philosophy as helping children to:

– be reflective about their own and other people's judgements
– improve reasoning
– strengthen personal judgements
– explore subtleties.
(Murris, 1992, p.3)

Oxfordshire schools which have used the Karen Murris approach have found it useful with all their pupils but particularly appealing for able pupils. It is often used when groups of able pupils are withdrawn from class to work together.

20. Book talk

This is Aiden Chambers' (1993) approach to encouraging useful discussion of fiction books. Many able pupils are avid readers but the opportunities to discuss their reading in depth are frequently limited. Structured discussion helps to develop critical analysis and also assists children in understanding why certain books are appealing or unappealing. It is interesting to note from Chambers' questions in Figure 3.20 that many of those in the general and special question categories make use of Bloom's higher order thinking, hence their usefulness in extension planning.

Summary

The creation of challenge in classroom planning should be a logical extension of general planning. It should avoid making able pupils do work in addition to that undertaken by others and be influenced by the principles outlined above. Outcomes for the most able should be clearly linked to the general learning outcomes for the lesson or module, and indeed extension is unlikely to be effective unless the module has expected learning outcomes. This kind of approach ensures effective continuity and progression and avoids the 'bolt-on' approach which characterizes so much extension work

---

Some of the 'Tell Me' questions

The Basic Questions
- Was there anything you liked about this book?
- Was there anything you disliked?
- Was there anything that puzzled you? ·
- Were there any patterns, any connections that you noticed?

The General Questions
- When you first saw the book, even before you read it, what kind of a book did you think it was going to be?
- Have you read other books like it?
- Have you read this book before? If so, was it different this time?
- While you were reading, or now when you think about it, were there words or phrases or other things to do with the language that you liked? Or didn't like?
- If the writer asked you what could be improved in the book, what would you say?
- Has anything that happens in the book ever happened to you?
- When you think about the book now, after all we've said, what is the most important thing about it for you?

The Special Questions
- How long did the story take to happen?
- Which characters interested you the most?
- Was there anyone not mentioned in the story but without whom it couldn't have happened?
- Think of yourself as a spectator. With whose eyes did you see the story? Did you only see what one character in the story saw, or did you see things sometimes as one character saw them and sometimes another?

Figures 3.20 'Book talk' questions

It is useful, when planning, to be aware of some of the approaches which are helpful in creating good extension work. Some of these approaches can be used with all pupils, some are only relevant to the most able, and some can be used by pupils of varying abilities if adapted appropriately. There is no single way to create good extension, but teachers need to develop an awareness of possible approaches which are well suited to the subject or age group of the pupils being taught.

Chapter 4

Classroom Provision

Introduction

In order to make any real sense of provision for able pupils in the classroom it is necessary to spend some time considering what we want for able children which is not already covered through good provision for all children. In some ways many of the things which we might want for our most able are in fact part of good provision for all children. Appropriate assessment and target-setting are an example of something that we might want for all pupils, but we may also need to consider their implications for the most able. However, there are some classroom issues which have particular importance in the education of the most able and these form the focus of this chapter.

Pace

The strategy which springs most readily to mind when first considering the needs of able pupils is allowing them to work more quickly than others – pace. Traditionally, able children have worked more quickly than others through the schools maths and reading schemes in primary schools and syllabi in secondary schools. Logic would suggest that this approach could be used with the National Curriculum; indeed the National Curriculum has been developed in such a way as to encourage pupils to progress through it at a rate which is suited to their ability. As a result of the Dearing Review, this approach was strengthened by the introduction of the 'access statement' which allows for the possibility of children working in a Key Stage beyond that expected for their age group.

> For the small number of pupils who may need the provision, material may be selected from earlier or later key stages where this is necessary to enable individual pupils to progress and demonstrate achievement. Such material should be presented in contexts suitable to the pupil's age. (DfEE, 1995)

Able pupils should work more quickly through any scheme of work or syllabus but this should not be the only approach to provision.

There are two main issues to be considered in the discussion of pace, one related to curriculum organization, the other to children's learning. The most important aspect to influence the pace debate is linked to children's learning. Too rapid a progression through a limited range of concepts and content is less effective in terms of learning than a more leisurely progression with time to *reflect, experiment and incubate ideas.*

Higher order thinking skills only come into play when children start to 'use and apply' their knowledge: hence the importance of AT1 in maths and science in providing extension opportunities. Learning is not just about acquiring new knowledge and comprehending it, it is about being able to utilize that information, linking it to other information in order to make generalizations, evaluating its relevance and effectiveness and presenting similar but new ideas based on what has been learnt. This is right at the heart of good provision for the most able. One of the advantages of working quickly through content and concepts which have to be covered is the chance to set some tasks which require these higher order skills. This is at least as valuable a learning experience as moving on to the next set of content or concepts to be covered.

From the organizational point of view, too heavy an emphasis on rapid progression means that matching work to the needs of the individual or group of pupils becomes increasingly difficult. In practice working in the next Key Stage presents huge problems in terms of both planning and resources. The teacher will need to explore and understand additional programmes of study in order to set work, and resources to support these programmes of study are unlikely to be readily available in the classroom. In addition, whilst it may be possible to support such an approach at an early stage of a child's schooling, the knock-on effect is considerable. It may prove very difficult for a Year 6 teacher to support work in Key Stage 3 in terms of expertise, and it may prove organizationally problematic for a secondary school to provide access to a higher Key Stage. Therefore, since one characteristic of good provision is that it should be sustainable throughout a child's schooling, manageability needs to be considered here. To quote a teacher:

> We all follow the same scheme of work (SOW) but with my most able I can cover things faster. This allows me to explore some things in more depth as we go along and usually we have time at the end to investigate something which is not in the SOW. This bit is often the most fun.

The subject area which presents the greatest problems in terms of pace is without doubt mathematics. Because maths is a conceptually-based, linear subject, it is possible for able mathematicians to make very rapid progress. Therefore this is the subject where one might reasonably expect to find individuals working at a level significantly in advance of their peers, i.e. in the next Key Stage.

Finally, there is the role of general classroom pace. One of the aspects which is most noticeable to me as I spend time in classrooms is the enormous variation in the pace of activity in different classrooms. It is very difficult for teachers in the normal course of their professional life to compare the pace in their classrooms with those of colleagues in their own and other schools. However, there is a strong case for the creation of this opportunity as part of a school's development work on able children.

Pace in classrooms varies from the slow and leisurely, through active and lively, and on to the pressured and frantic. This issue may seem at first to be peripheral to the needs of able pupils but in fact it is crucial to their high achievement. Slow leisurely classrooms, whilst often very caring and warm, usually have underachieving able pupils. In short, although these children could achieve more, they are unlikely to do so unless someone ups the pace. In active lively classrooms, able pupils are usually aware of the shape of the day and the expected time-scale for their piece of work. This, as well as keeping them on task, allows them to make a decision, for example, to work harder and negotiate for some time to do an activity of their choice. Greater independence often develops in these circumstances. Of course too rapid a pace or over-ambitious expectations can lead to stress. Able pupils in these circumstances can find themselves 'doing' frantically and thinking little.

In schools where pace is very rapid, perhaps another focus for school discussion is whether a desire to cover the National Curriculum content sometimes leads to unrealistic planning for the time available. Classrooms rarely experience a whole day without unforeseen interruptions. Yet in most schools planning is done on the assumption that everything will occur in the time planned. A university research colleague when working with me on a primary school research project noted: 'It seems there is no such thing as a normal day in a primary school. Every time we visit one something unexpected is happening'. If this is the reality, then we need to plan with this in mind. Perhaps it would help us as teachers to avoid that feeling of things running out of control.

So, to summarize the pace debate: if able pupils are to be successful they need to be actively engaged with their learning but not constantly racing through tasks in order to complete as many as possible. The pace should be brisk but there should also be opportunities to stop and reflect. Pupils need to recognize what they have learnt as well as what has been taught. Planning should exist for tasks which require children to use and reflect on their new learning before they move on to another set of concepts or content.

High teacher expectation

Much has been said by HMI and OFSTED about the link between high teacher expectation and high standards. 'High expectations are a crucial characteristic of virtually all unusually effective schools described in case studies' (Levine and Lezotte, in Sammons *et al.*, 1996, p.17)

The difficulty for the class teacher lies in understanding what is meant. For the most able, high teacher expectation is arguably more important than for any other group. A low expectation on the part of the teacher, or the school generally, may well contribute to the under-achievement of able pupils.

It is interesting to explore why low teacher expectation may occur. Clearly, if everyone were in agreement that high expectations were important and unproblematic, then low teacher expectation would not occur. Perhaps low expectation occurs by omission or accident, or perhaps through some muddled educational thinking. Some reasons for low expectation are as follows:

- poor assessment of individuals' capabilities;
- lack of clarity about learning outcomes;

- assumptions based on gender or class;
- a desire to ensure that no child fails;
- lack of differentiation;
- a focus on curriculum access at the expense of high achievement.

Poor assessment of individuals' capabilities

There is a very close link between good assessment and high performance. From the point of view of the most able, this is because what might reasonably be considered appropriate for the majority may be too easy for the most able. However, unless a clear picture is available of the child's previous performance, it is difficult to identify the level at which to pitch the harder work. An additional problem here is that the teacher needs to identify what the 'harder work' might look like. It is arguably easier to tackle a learning difficulty than a learning strength. If a pupil experiences a difficulty you do at least know what you are aiming towards. For the most able, the teacher has to identify a route forward and make decisions on work to be tackled.

Much assessment is based on whether a child can or cannot do particular things, or has/has not covered particular things. This kind of approach is unhelpful for able pupils because it does not give credit for doing things excessively well or indeed at an unexpectedly early age. An example of this might be reading on entry into reception. The assessment might ask such questions as, can the child recognize letters? Can the child recognize whole words? Can the child read simple sentences? This may well be perfectly adequate for most children but it does not allow for the child who is already an accomplished reader and whose reading needs fall far outside what might normally be expected in the reception classroom. Therefore the teacher may have low expectations of the child's abilities.

Lack of clarity about learning outcomes

Often when short-term planning is done in school the main focus is on the activities which the pupils will undertake and the resources which might be needed to support these activities. The learning outcomes are not always clearly stated, but these are in fact essential to ensuring high achievement. The teacher needs to be clear about what they hope children are to learn generally if they are to stand any chance of identifying more sophisticated outcomes for the most able. Low expectation occurs when either the teacher puts a ceiling on the task (i.e., 'This is what you do and when you have completed it you move on to something else'), or when the teacher is not clear about the learning inherent in the task and therefore the possible progression routes.

This is particularly relevant in open-ended tasks. Unless the teacher has a feel for a range of possible outcomes then low level outcomes can occur. An example of this might be a maths investigation. Whilst some progress can be made by simply exploring the problem, the teacher may need to lead or prompt children if they are to move beyond this into algebraic notation or mathematical generalizations. Otherwise it is a rather like giving a child Lego and saying, 'Now build something'. You may get a masterpiece but you are more likely to get a limited outcome.

Assumptions based on gender or class

It is a sad reflection on the teaching profession that teachers habitually equate able children with the white middle classes. On my taking up an LEA post with responsibility for able pupils, a headteacher colleague whose views and opinions I generally respect joked: 'Well we won't be needing your help, we don't have any of those kind of children in my school'. This was an inner-city school which prided itself on the quality of its work with children. However, it clearly had low expectations of what the children might achieve, simply based on the home background.

Experience shows that if you do not expect to find any able pupils in the school then you do not find them. This is because it is unlikely that opportunities will have been made available which would allow for the identification or recognition of ability. *All schools have some able children. It is the task of the school to recognize ability and to nurture it.*

It is arguably more important for the school to recognize ability in situations where such ability might otherwise be overlooked, than in middle-class areas where parents' expectations influence the school agenda. Linda Evans, in *Degrees of Disadvantage* (1995) raises some interesting issues related to able children in inner-city schools and highlights some of the reasons why teachers' high expectations can make a significant difference to the lives of individuals.

In all schools issues of gender, race and class need to be considered. Questions related to identification are more fully covered in Chapter 2, but a school should review its register of able children to consider issues of equality of opportunity. What percentage of those recognized are boys, have English as a second language, or come from disadvantaged homes?

Desire to ensure that no child fails

Primary classrooms in particular have traditionally been a place where children are provided with a secure learning environment in which to achieve. Sometimes the pursuit of this laudable aim has led to low expectations on the part of the teacher. This usually occurs for one of two reasons. First, a desire to ensure that all pupils can tackle a task may mean that the teacher sets it at an artificially low level. This results in the task no longer being well matched to the needs of the most able. Second, there is a desire to ensure that the task is not too challenging for the most able. This may lead to excessive caution. In fact able pupils need to tackle tasks which make them struggle and occasionally even fail, otherwise they never learn the strategies for coping with difficulty and may find failure very traumatic at a later stage of their educational development.

An appropriate classroom climate can allow the teacher to aim high for all children. In a classroom where risk-taking and hypothesizing are highly valued, regardless of the end outcome, then children are more comfortable with the idea of failing to complete a task. There are also some interesting teaching techniques to enable a teacher to aim high. This example happened in a Year 1 classroom:

The teacher had the class seated on the carpet and was about to introduce the lesson. She looked at them for a moment and then announced that, on reflection, she thought that the lesson she had planned may prove to be too difficult and that she should revise it. The children were adamant. 'No, no we can do it, we will have a go at it', etc. She tried again, reiterating that it would be a struggle for them. They were unmoveable! They would do it.

This was a clever approach on the part of the teacher in that she had provided them with a safety net. If they failed, well, that was to be expected: but if they succeeded they would be very pleased with themselves.

Lack of differentiation

This is a difficult area in any classroom. In recent years most teachers have developed a range of skills and strategies for ensuring appropriate differentiation for pupils with SEN. Indeed this has been formalized through the target-setting and Individual Education Plans of the *Code of Practice*. Training, resources and structures are much less available for the most able, and classroom differentiation is consequently less well developed.

Lack of appropriate differentiation does lead to under-achievement in able children and classroom differentiation is the single most important issue for any school to tackle if they are to improve their provision for this group.

A focus on curriculum access at the expense of high achievement

Both in my research work with Mary Fuller (Eyre and Fuller, 1993) and in inservice generally, teachers have expressed guilt about time spent working with able children. Children who have learning or behaviour problems are perceived as having greater needs. This issue is not about who has or has not a right to teacher time but rather an equality of opportunity issue. *All children, regardless of ability have a right to an appropriate education. It is the duty of every school to ensure that no child's needs are overlooked because of the needs of others.*

Classroom management and teacher time

The most valuable resource in the classroom is the teacher. For able pupils, time with the teacher is just as important as it is for other pupils. Able children may seem capable of executing tasks, but they still need adult help if they are to take their learning forward. Whilst able children should be encouraged to be independent and to develop their own approaches to problems, their need for teacher time is in no way diminished. They do not need a teacher to be with them to enable them to access tasks, but they do need a teacher to help them develop tasks and evaluate their work.

HMI, in its survey, *Education Observed: The education of very able children in maintained schools* (1992, p.viii) stated that: 'The judicious intervention of the teacher to urge pupils to a higher level of knowledge, skill, understanding and thinking was crucial'. This is particularly interesting observation because, in practice, the most able pupils in a classroom are usually the ones who receive the least teacher time. In conversation with teachers, this is generally attributed to the heavy demand on teacher time from other children:

> The most able can usually get on on their own, so I tend to spend time with those who need help to do the task. Also, some individually demanding children take up a lot of time. If everyone is settled then I try to spend some time with the most able.

Whilst this approach is in many ways understandable it does not lead to effective provision for able children. My own research into Year 6 classrooms supports the notion that quality teacher time is, for the most able, a rare commodity. In all the classrooms we studied (Eyre and Fuller, 1993, p.14) certain factors remained constant, regardless of size or nature of school:

- Able pupils received very little one-to-one time with the teacher.
- Able pupils rarely asked for help from their teachers.
- Pupils often asked each other for help.
- Pupils were enthusiastic about all work, even the most mundane.

Clearly these findings are a cause for some concern. HMI suggests that one-to-one time with the teacher is important, yet this was not a feature of any of the classrooms we observed. The lack of interaction between the most able and their teachers may be partly explained by the actions of the children themselves. The signals which they gave did not invite teacher intervention, i.e., they did not look 'stuck', and since most teachers are very busy in the classroom they may have read this as a sign that they were not needed. It is particularly significant that the children were enthusiastic about all tasks, even dull ones. This is not an unusual finding and is borne out by a variety of general research into primary education (e.g., Bennett *et al.*, 1984). However, it does mean that a teacher cannot rely on expressions of dissatisfaction as an indicator that the work is badly matched to the needs of pupils. This may be a crucial reason why so many schools have a lack of appropriate provision identified as a key issue in OFSTED inspections.

Most able children will not become disruptive if under-challenged; they just carry out the task. They may however complain of being bored.

If it is acknowledged that in order to improve provision for able pupils the teacher will need to spend more time with the most able, then the question of how that can realistically be achieved must be addressed. Clearly in large classes this is a difficult problem because time for the most able should not be achieved at the expense of other pupils. However, much can be achieved by a closer look at ways to maximize 'teacher time'. Issues which a school might usefully consider include:

- classroom layout and management;
- use of adults;
- teacher explanation and questioning;
- marking and evaluation;
- resources;
- whole-class teaching.

Classroom layout and management

Well-organized teachers seem to have much more time to spend discussing learning with their pupils. In their classes pupils know where to go when they come in, where equipment is kept, which equipment can be accessed without asking the teacher and which books and/or paper they use for particular tasks. In some classrooms, especially in Key Stage 1, much of the routine and organization may be done by the teacher or another adult. Young children are in fact well able to organize themselves in the classroom and requiring them to do so helps them become more independent in their approach to learning. Many nursery classes establish classroom routines very effectively, but these are not always maintained as the children move through the school. Many Year 6 teachers expect their pupils to be highly independent while Year 7 teachers expect a high level of dependency.

An exploration of the tasks which pupils might reasonably be asked to undertake for the teacher is a useful way to avoid time spent on low level tasks. Giving children classroom jobs is one way to encourage leadership qualities and can also be helpful in raising the self-esteem of individuals. One aspect of providing for the most able is the recognition of achievement in a broad range of areas. Outstanding organizers can be recognized and rewarded through being given responsibility in the school or classroom, and this is helpful in the drive to ensure that abilities beyond the academic are given recognition in the classroom.

A useful staff discussion could focus on ways in which individual teachers organize and run their classrooms. Do pupils experience very different approaches when they change teacher? Does it matter?

Use of adults

Most primary schools are fortunate in having a range of adults working in the school on a voluntary or paid basis. Teacher time can be freed by making maximum use of adults in the classroom. From the point of view of able children, non-teaching adults can be used in a variety of ways; the most obvious is making use of any particular skills or abilities which the adult might have. If you are fortunate enough to have an adult with particular expertise or background then they might take a group on a regular basis.

In one class of Year 4 children a parent-helper was a worker with Oxfam. She had a small group for six hours, spread over half a term. They worked on a project considering the sale of crops, from the price paid to the third-world farmer to the price in the local supermarket. This was part of the class's general work on a Key Stage 2 comparative study of life in the Gambia and Britain. This work was very challenging for the children involved but also very stimulating and encouraged the children to reflect upon some deeper issues than the ones being covered by the class as a whole. However, this work was not done in isolation and the group's findings were presented to the whole class for discussion and debate.

Of course not every adult is able to bring particular expertise or indeed is confident enough to take a group in that way. There are a range of other ways in which adults can support the work of able children without actually bringing particular expertise of their own. Many of the higher level challenges set for children require discussion, debate and decision making. However, not all children, even at the top of Key Stage 2, have the maturity to work well in a group. It is particularly difficult to work in a group when the task is open and the outcome not predetermined, and some able children cannot cope with this. The use of an adult to chair rather than lead the discussion can allow a group of immature able children to tackle a challenging group task without the help of the teacher.

Another possibility is to use the adult to give certain types of help to the group. In this approach the teacher decides what kind of help the group can have and what must be done alone. It is often a problem that non-teachers working with able children tend to give them more help and guidance than they really need, especially in Key Stage 1 classrooms. If you want the group to work either alone or as a team but need an adult to supervise, then it is helpful to identify the kinds of help the adult can give. This encourages the children to think and develop independence without the activity degenerating into chaos.

Finally the teacher can work with a small group of able children while the adult helps other pupils. The teacher working with a small group for a time, when others cannot interrupt, is a method used frequently in primary schools to ensure quality teacher time. (It is sometimes described as a 'bubble' approach. The teacher is in the bubble with the group and no other member of the class is allowed to break the bubble.) This technique works more easily if another adult is available to field questions from other pupils in the class.

Teacher explanation and questioning

One of the characteristics of many able children is that they like to see the big picture. It enables them to make connections between one set of information and another and may help to clarify their thinking. *When children have the chance to share in the teacher's planning, those with ability will become apparent.*

It appears that where able pupils understand very clearly both what is required of them and why, they are able to explore the activity thoroughly and may reach more innovative conclusions. My observations of able pupils in school lead me to conclude that when there are a range of possible ways to approach a task, able children tend to take the teacher into account in making their selection. So, in a class where the teacher sets great store by doing things right, the child will probably choose a safe but possibly unspectacular route. In a class where the children are privy to the broader agenda they are able to determine whether their more unusual or innovative response meets the criteria.

A Year 3/4 class in a village school were working on the sinking of the Mary Rose. Their task for this session was to work in groups and to create a newspaper front page covering the story from a variety of different angles. They were told to write their articles from the viewpoints of: a survivor, a person watching from the dockside, and the relative of a drowned sailor. In the most able group the discussion of the activity led to a consideration of who could really be blamed for the disaster. The children felt that in their newspaper they really should interview the architect since his design seemed to be unstable. This they did, and used the computer to do layout design, all without consulting their teacher. When I questioned them about this they were very clear as to the purpose of the task and assured me that since their interpretation did not deviate from the purpose it would be acceptable to the teacher. Indeed as one child explained, 'She likes you to change the task and add your own ideas'.

This encouragement of innovation and risk-taking often leads to high quality work and does not require additional teacher time.

Questioning plays an important role in developing children's thinking. It can prompt them into thinking in a different way or into considering additional information. However, much of the questioning that occurs in class is still very closed and more designed to establish whether children have grasped particular facts than to explore their thinking. In Wragg and Brown's book, *Questioning* (1993) they identify a useful list of probing questions (see Figure 4 .1). These are very helpful in both determining a child's current thinking and in moving their thinking forward.

Examples of probing questions

Does that always apply?
Can you give me an example of that?
How does that fit in (relevance)?
You say it is X, which particular kind of X?
What are the exceptions?
Why do you think that is true?
Is there another view?
What is the idea behind that?
Can you tell me the difference between the two?

Note These examples may be modified in various ways. They are presented here
only to give the flavour of the skill of probing and not to provide a
mechanical checklist of all the different approaches to probing.

Figure 4.1 Wragg and Brown's questions

Marking and evaluation

Assessment is extremely important in determining the appropriate level of work for children. In the case of able pupils this is particularly important if a good match between ability and work set is to be achieved. Able pupils are capable of assessing and evaluating their own work and they should be encouraged to develop these skills, and also to learn from each piece useful lessons for the future. Good quality marking allows pupils to understand more clearly the assessment criteria being applied to their work and therefore helps them to identify an agenda for improvement. If a pupil does not understand why a piece of work has been given a good or bad mark then it is difficult for him or her to decide on ways to improve. What may seem obvious to us as adults may not be quite so obvious to a child.

Therefore sharing the criteria for assessment with pupils before they start an activity has much to commend it. This allows comments to be linked to the agreed criteria and allows the child to reflect more thoughtfully on the comments made. Some teachers have developed this in a formal way. An American example I came across specified what a child needs to do to obtain medium and high grades. For my taste this example was too contrived but the idea is an interesting one.

The whole question of assessment and marking requires some sensitive handling otherwise it can become cumbersome and ineffective. For example, as a general approach it is helpful for comments on children's work to include a target for the future. However, if this becomes a standard pattern then the pupil never experiences that rewarding feeling of having done a really good piece of work. The positive comments are tempered with 'but next time'. A Year 8 describing this to me one day said, 'It does not matter how hard you try, or how good your work is, she always finds something to complain about!'

Resources

The availability of appropriate resources to support extension tasks is crucial to high achievement. However, careful consideration needs to be given to choosing resources if they are to be effective in extending the learning of able pupils. It is easy to assume that able pupils need resources which have been specially written for them. This is not always the case and those which have been written for able children are not always of good quality.

At the present time few publishers produce resources for able children. Some extension opportunities are offered in commercial schemes, especially maths schemes, but there is little related to topic work or humanities. Resources targeted at able children are generally either of the cross-curricular/problem-solving variety or one-off ideas which are not linked to general classroom planning. Both of these groups are useful in a limited way but are peripheral to the work that is at the heart of day-to-day classroom teaching. It is helpful for a school to have these types of tasks available to offer when other work is finished as they help to develop logical and lateral thinking, but they are not the only resource needed. NACE (at Westminster College, Oxford) keeps up-to-date information on available resources of this type since they are often produced through individual LEAs.

Other resources are of a more general nature. All classroom should include resources which assume different learning levels in the classroom. We are all familiar with the idea of easier dictionaries and reference books for those who have difficulty accessing text, but this should be balanced by harder (perhaps adult) dictionaries, atlases and information books for those who can manage difficult text. It is pointless attempting to develop research skills as part of extension planning if the books available to research from are simplistic and too few in number to allow comparative study. When discussing this question of the range of books with an early years colleague, she remarked:

> If we are serious about saying that we should have picture books available in Year 6 classrooms, then we should also be providing chapter books in the nursery for those who want to read sustained text.

Other useful resources include any which use an investigative, problem-solving approach. These are likely to require pupils to use higher level thinking skills and so are well suited to able children. Such books are not restricted to maths and science; a careful look at educational catalogues will yield examples in the humanities, languages, etc. Some publishers, for example Tarquin Books and Clare Publications, specialize in this kind of approach and it is worth keeping an eye on their lists. *In short the classroom should contain resources, books and equipment in the expectation that some children will access higher conceptual levels. Often there is a ceiling on learning because the teacher does not have readily available the equipment needed to demonstrate the next concept or idea.*

The housing or locating of resources is a difficult issue for schools. In the secondary school, lessons which are taught in departmental bases have access to a wider range of resources than those taught in other parts of the school. In primary schools, questions related to the location of resources are focused on sharing. Should the full range of resources be housed in each classroom with the resultant financial implications? What messages does it send if a child has to go to class of older children to get books or equipment? Is a general school store a realistic possibility?

Whole-class teaching

At first glance it seems unlikely that whole-class teaching might be an effective way to meet the needs of the most able. Indeed in many primary classrooms the management of discussion is particularly difficult when a wide ability range exists. Able children often want to move on faster and to go into greater depth than most other children and this can lead to their domination of discussions or disruptive behaviour. An astute Year 3 girl analysed the problem thus:

> My teacher doesn't like me to put my hand up in discussions. I know this because when she asks a question she always looks at everyone else first and then if no one else puts their hand up she asks me. I think she is embarrassed because I know too many of the answers. So I've decided to help her. I now only put up my hand every third question or so.

This tension, coupled with other issues, does lead many teachers in primary schools to avoid whole-class teaching as much as possible. From the perspective of able children, whole-class teaching can be quite useful. If there is a new area to be addressed, e.g. a new programme of study in history or geography, and if some of the core can be covered as a class lesson, it allows able children to move rapidly into extension activities. This working as a class also means that even if subsequently children will undertake different tasks, there is less sense of fragmentation.

Whole-class teaching is also one way to ensure that able children experience a greater proportion of actual teaching. As has been mentioned previously, much group work is, for able children, largely unsupported; whole-class teaching does allow for greater interaction with the teacher. In my opinion, the fact that all of the lesson may not be strictly necessary for able pupils is less of a problem than might be supposed. A little careful questioning by the teacher or a discussion prior to the lesson regarding the extension tasks to follow, can mean that the most able have to interpret the class lesson in a more sophisticated way. Even if this is not possible, the most able will probably do their own thinking during the lesson, especially if independent thinking is generally encouraged and valued by the teacher.

Finally, some of the best lessons I see are when a teacher is teaching the whole class about something he or she enjoys. This is the craft of teaching at its best. Good teachers are able to juggle demand, to extend some and support others, while still following their planned agenda. A certain intellectual excitement is created in these circumstances which is difficult to replicate in any other form. So whole-class teaching, as part of the full range of teaching styles, has a valuable role to play.

Who does extension?

Most people looking at provision for able pupils assume that you will identify a group of children who will benefit from extension and then plan the extension tasks to meet their needs. In practice this is extremely difficult to do and limited in its effectiveness. Pupils frequently surprise you by their response to a task and it is difficult to say with any real certainty who will be able to tackle the harder work. Pupils also dislike those kind of decisions being taken on their behalf. For example, Becky (Year 6) stated:

> The people who my teacher thought were good at English went out of class to do poetry. I really like poetry but I wasn't chosen because I'm not much good at spelling. Carla was and she didn't even want to go.

This view warrants some sympathy. Motivation is as important as innate ability and Becky may well have benefited more from the opportunity than Carla.

These thoughts and concerns have led to my viewing the whole process in reverse, an approach which I have found to be infinitely more helpful and effective. Plan the extension tasks first and then decide who will do them. This approach has several advantages. First, it leads to easier and more logical extension planning. It allows you to consider the task and then look at how it could be extended. This will probably be linked to concepts which other pupils will cover later and which you can show through assessment have been covered by some children at this point. It may be that the extension concerns the using and applying of the concept being learnt, and once again it is possible to log that experience as part of the assessment process.

Another advantage is the opportunity to manage the extension in a way that best suits the situation. Sometimes when an extension has been planned you realize that in fact quite a lot of pupils could tackle it, especially if some have additional support, and so this may become a whole-class extension, raising teacher expectation. On other occasions it is clearly only applicable to those with particular skills and therefore you may group by ability.

This way of working allows for a significant number of pupils to experience extension and avoids the creation of an elite group. It recognizes the breadth and diversity of talent in the average classroom.

Learning outcomes

Learning outcomes are what you expect pupils to learn from the task or tasks. In the case of the most able you might expect them to:

- take the concept further,
- explore the idea more broadly,
- interpret the same task differently,
- learn an additional concept.

These expected learning outcomes for the most able can act as aides-mémoire for busy teachers who are planning extension.

Summary

Classroom provision for the most able is best achieved by building on existing classroom structures. Teachers need to be alert to the difficulties related to pace and to the management of teacher time. They need to create a classroom climate which expects excellence from all pupils and where children's achievements are valued and rewarded.

Extension should become a classroom habit with both teacher and children expecting to extend the basic task. Extension should not be the exclusive domain of a specially selected group but an opportunity for anyone who shows themselves able enough and motivated enough to accomplish the task.

Chapter 5

Issues for Secondary Schools

Introduction

The management of provision in the secondary sector is surprisingly similar regardless of the nature of the school involved. Even within a highly selective school some pupils will be more able than others, and need particular consideration. In this kind of school the range of ability within the cohort is reduced but is still significant. Selective schools that target their school provision towards one particular element of their cohort encounter similar problems to comprehensive schools. A number of OFSTED reports on selective schools have identified lack of challenge for the most able as a 'key issue'. In these schools the focus has been towards the majority, with less concern for the most able – a problem in common with comprehensive schools, except that the majority in the selective school is working at a higher level.

Comprehensive schools form the major focus of this book because the vast majority of pupils are educated in them. However, any school may undertake development work based on this process simply by looking at its most able pupils. Certainly this kind of approach has been used by colleagues in special schools or units as well as highly selective schools.

The school culture

Perhaps the biggest obstacles to effective provision for able pupils are school and pupil attitudes. It is not considered 'cool' to be bright. This attitude is usually assumed to be found only in the comprehensive system but is a factor in even the most selective schools. This is because culturally the English have an ambivalent response to success. In sporting terms, success is acceptable although preferred in teams rather than individual achievement. Too much individual success is seen as making people big-headed. Academic success is less commonly valued. High achievers attempt to make little of their success for fear of being seen as arrogant, and the English language even includes terms of abuse linked to success – 'smart Alec' and 'clever clogs'. Worse still is being seen to try hard. Somehow it is more acceptable to succeed if success comes without trying, hence even adults make light of the effort involved in reaching their goal.

This type of cultural attitude has a significant impact on the life of a school. If success is not valued by their peer group and the larger public then it not surprising that many pupils do not see success as essential or even, in some cases, desirable. Equally, if the world at large does not admit that in order to be successful one has to work hard, then children are unlikely to see trying as important.

Schools have in their own way inadvertently added to this problem. They often do not reward achievement and seem much more comfortable recognizing progress in all pupils. Whilst this does have a part to play, able pupils often perceive that they should not be seen to achieve too highly, and therefore achieve at a level which they think will be more acceptable. This leads to acceptable standards but underachieving pupils.

Effective schools and able pupils

Much research has been undertaken in recent years into identifying the characteristics of effective schools. This has resulted in the publication of materials for heads and senior managers which highlight key areas. Sammons *et al.* (1996) in their list (see Figure 5.1) nominate a series of factors which are significant for schools generally but also for able child provision.

If a school is to be deemed a 'good school', then it must provide an effective education for *all* its pupils. It is possible for a school to be a good school for the majority of its pupils but not be effective in challenging its most able. This is amply demonstrated by OFSTED inspection reports which, at the same time as identifying the school as a good one, note lack of challenge as an issue in most or even all of the subject reports. Therefore adherence to the body of research on effective schools will not, in itself, ensure good provision for the most able. However, school effectiveness and particularly school improvement work does have significance for work on able pupils. Conversely, able pupil work has an impact on school improvement.

School effectiveness work and school improvement work are significant for able pupil provision because it is impossible for a school to be a good school for able pupils unless it is already a good school. Schools which try to improve their provision for the most able whilst still having ineffective general systems are unlikely to be successful. This is because provision for the most able is an extension of existing systems, e.g. if systematic departmental planning is not well established then it is impossible for that department to achieve effective extension planning. However, when a school is looking towards improvement, it is helpful to target one element of school provision as the vehicle for improving general provision. There is a strong case for suggesting that able pupils may be a good target group. Burntwood School, Wandsworth, is an example of this approach; its achievements are recorded in *Success against the Odds* (National Commission on Education, 1996). A focus on the most able led to an examination of all major school systems and a subsequent raising of achievement.

A growing body of evidence is emerging to suggest that if a school looks systematically at its provision for the most able, then overall school standards will rise. This link was first

ELEVEN FACTORS FOR EFFECTIVE SCHOOLS	
1 **Professional leadership**	Firm and purposeful A participative approach The leading professional
2 **Shared vision and goals**	Unity of purpose Consistency of practices Collegiality and collaboration
3 **A learning environment**	An orderly atmosphere An attractive working environment
4 **Concentration on teaching and learning**	Maximisation of learning time Academic emphasis Focus on achievement
5 **Purposeful teaching**	Efficient organisation Clarity of purpose Structured lessons Adaptive practice
6 **High expectations**	High expectations all round Communicating expectations Providing intellectual challenge
7 **Positive reinforcement**	Clear and fair discipline Feedback
8 **Monitoring progress**	Monitoring pupil performance Evaluating school performance
9 **Pupil rights and responsibilities**	Raising pupil self-esteem Positions of responsibility Control of work
10 **Home-school partnership**	Parental involvement in their children's learning
11 **A learning organisation**	School-based staff development

Figure 5.1 Eleven factors for effective schools

recorded by HMI in 1992 and confirmed by OFSTED at the 1995 Berkshire Headteachers' Conference: 'If you are willing to deal effectively with the needs of able pupils you will raise the standards of all pupils'.

The NACE/DfEE project (1996) also makes reference to this in its anecdotal evidence from 50 networks of teachers throughout the country. The reason for this link is likely to be the focus on subject-specific aptitude rather than on general intelligence. In Oxfordshire comprehensive schools, approximately 40 per cent of pupils are identified when teachers are asked to nominate the 10 per cent most able pupils on a subject-by-subject basis. A focus therefore, on challenging the most able which includes a departmental element, is likely to affect a significant percentage of the school cohort and influence overall achievement. Systematic research into this link has not yet been undertaken but small-scale research plus league table results lend weight to this theory.

Commitment

One of the greatest problems in improving any aspect of provision in schools is gaining commitment from the whole staff. This is particularly difficult in the area of provision for able pupils. Resistance to a focus on the most able is not restricted to professional dissension but is part of a wider political and cultural question. Alexander *et al.* (1992, p.32) said:

> In some schools and local education authorities the legitimate drive to create equal opportunities for all has resulted in an obsessive fear of anything which, in the jargon, might be deemed 'elitist'. As a result the needs of some of our most able children have quite simply not been met.

This view continues to exist amongst many individual teachers who consider able pupils to be educationally advantaged and unworthy of any special attention. There lurks here an assumption that able pupils will always do well and that others are more deserving of attention. This view is incorrect and must be addressed by any senior management team seeking to improve provision for the most able. If a school, as the 1988 Education Act states, is to provide an appropriate education for *all* its pupils then provision for the most able becomes a question of equality of opportunity. If a school does not make appropriate provision then able pupils are not receiving their entitlement. Extensive research evidence indicates that schools do make a difference to the achievements of able pupils; rather than automatic achievement, lack of provision leads to underachievement and possible disruptive behaviour (Freeman, 1991; Montgomery, 1996).

Even amongst staff who see a need to provide for able pupils, the guilt factor is immense. In inservice work nationally, this is a consistent message from teachers. They feel guilty about any time spent with able pupils because other pupils may be achieving at such a low level. This is an issue for discussion. Are able pupils not entitled to teacher time and consideration? If they are not then why are they bothering to come to school? A school emphasis on drawing all pupils up to an acceptable level (raising standards) may lead to able pupils being ignored. The senior management team may need to address this question of fair distribution of teacher time, otherwise well-meaning teachers may continue to ignore the most able.

Finally, as regards commitment, there is the recognition of the need for realism. Research suggests that consistency of viewpoint may be the most difficult aspect to achieve. Staff may agree to developments at the time of planning but may be less willing to make real changes when the time for implementation occurs. In addition, new staff will not have been part of the decision-making process and may be expected to have the usual range of prejudices in respect of able pupils. Senior management will need to remind staff frequently of the rationale behind provision for the most able, if useful work is to be achieved.

A school policy for able pupils

The main purpose behind a policy for able pupils is to record the school's aims in respect of these pupils and the systems through which provision for able pupils is made. Because of the size and nature of secondary schools, provision for the most able will be a partial responsibility for a number of staff, in addition to a coordinator for able pupils. The vast majority of provision will be made in subject departments through both curriculum differentiation and curriculum enhancement. However, there is also a whole-school element to this in the shape of clubs/societies and school productions.

Some schools list their opportunities for able pupils as part of a leaflet to parents. This is useful in two respects. First, it sends a clear message to parents that able pupils are valued within the school and that provision for them does exist. Second, it helps the school to gain an overall picture of the range of opportunities on offer, in the categories of both enrichment (breadth of opportunity) and extension (depth). A more subtle effect of such a leaflet is the impact on departments. No department wants to be seen as having little on offer and so it may extend its range of opportunities. The list in Figure 5.2 is an example from Henry Box School, Witney.

Many good booklets now exist to assist schools in devising school policy for able pupils, including *Writing a School Policy* (Teare, 1996) and *Supporting More Able Pupils* (O'Connell, 1996). My own pro forma for policy writing can be found in Appendix 1, and an exemplar policy from Marston Middle School, Oxford in Appendix 2.

The most important aspect of school policy for able pupils is that it should be an effective reflection of provision. Policy which simply outlines the desirable and fails to link it to the actual is of little real value. If a school offers really good provision for able pupils it is actually quite difficult to identify all the provision. A key tenet for most schools is that provision is integral rather than 'bolt-on'. This makes for effective provision but also tends to obscure provision.

Example

In one school, work placements take account of pupils' abilities, and staff work to ensure that the most able have appropriate work placements. This is technically part of the school's provision but in this instance provision for the most able is so well grounded in the school that everything that the school does takes account of the most able. Hence it becomes difficult to identify all areas of provision. This school has excellent provision but its components are difficult to identify. The policy here refers to the way in which all aspects of school provision reflect the full range of pupils and gives relevant examples of provision rather than attempting to identify all of it. This school has moved beyond the early stages of able pupil provision (spotting existing provision and identifying areas of new provision) to a truly permeative model. This is a significant move forward, but as with all permeative models there exists the possibility of able pupil provision ceasing to exist. This is provision at its best but also needs careful regulation and monitoring to ensure its continued existence.

THE HENRY BOX SCHOOL
Extension and Enrichment Courses for More Able Pupils 1994

Chemistry Competition Top sets of Year 9 science have been invited to participate in a national competition. Regional finals will take place in July at Brookes University; national finals in September in London. An enrichment course will extend the pupils' knowledge and experience of practical chemistry. Participants will be asked to attend a weekly 'Chemistry Club' and take part in two 'egg races' as well as preparing and delivering a practical demonstration. The course leader is Ms Exon.

Residential Course Mrs Payne has expressed an interest in running a critical art course for selected pupils. These may be selected according to intellectual ability not necessary artistic ability.

English Enrichment Enrichment and extension programmes are being developed for more able students.

Contacts with Industry A visit has been arranged by Ms Goggin for Year 10 physics students to 'Oxford Instruments' in the Easter term.

Mathematics Challenge An intermediate challenge is taking place in February and Year 10 pupils will have received letters inviting them to take part. Some out of school commitment will be required. The junior challenge finals will take place in March. The Senior competition, which involves 6th form students, took place on November 9th. This is organised by Ms Collin.

Latin Pupils who have successfully taken the Latin taster course in Year 8 are now into their first term of study of their Latin GCSE course. The course tutor is Mrs R Edy. Year 8 pupils will be invited to sample the introduction to the Cambridge Latin Course. Those who demonstrate an aptitude for the subject may then continue to study to GCSE level.

Youth Award Scheme This is a nationally accredited scheme which acknowledges and rewards the basic skills of individual pupils. The award is made at Bronze, Silver, Gold and Platinum level, the latter being regarded on a par with GCSE and A Level respectively. This scheme will be launched with a targeted group of pupils before January. Pupils will be developing a twinning scheme with a school in Bolivia. This project will have direct relevance to the whole school cross curricula topic, 'South America'. This scheme will be led by Mrs Macmillan.

Withdrawal Sessions These will take place during the Easter term and will run during the school day. One will be based on the use of words and their derivatives; the other will be a practical problem solving activity.

Chess The school Chess Club flourishes. It provides a focus for pupils of all abilities and ages to pursue an intellectual activity. Chess Club is run by Mrs Macmillan.

S K Macmillan. Learning Support Department

Figure 5.2 Whole school activities: an example

Organizational systems

A major consideration for headteachers and managers in the secondary school is the question of school organization. Much has been said recently regarding the value of fast-tracking, streaming and setting and many schools are reassessing their organizational structures. For able pupils such organizational structures may be less influential than is often supposed. How the system is mediated is often more important than the system itself. If a setted class is whole-class taught all the time and little consideration given to the needs of individuals, then it is certainly no more effective than a well planned mixed-ability class. *Particularly in the case of comprehensive schools, grouping and organization are important in ensuring that able pupils are challenged, but they will not in themselves ensure effective provision.*

Fast-tracking

This term is used to mean an express route through traditional schooling both for cohorts and for individuals. Mathematics is the subject within which most fast-tracking occurs. Cohorts of pupils may take GCSE a year early and individuals may do GCSE and A Level a number of years in advance of their peers. Fast-tracking by a cohort of pupils clearly has some advantages. Mathematics, in particular, is a conceptually-based subject and pupils with mathematical flair can make rapid progress. Students, having gained their GCSE early, can move on to A-Level work and university modules. Whether this has any long-term advantages for individuals is questionable; even most grammar schools reject fast-tracking and for comprehensive schools there is the question of whether enough is gained by this to warrant the disruption caused to the rest of the school.

Often a fast-track cohort does not easily identify itself. Perhaps 15 or so pupils are obvious candidates and either they are taught as a group and other group sizes increased to accommodate all other pupils in the year, or the top group remains its usual size, with segments of the class finding the pace too rapid. These pupils may get a less advantageous mark when taking maths a year early than if they had taken the exam with the rest of their year. Other problems include the 'knock-on' effect of fast-tracking. In order for these pupils to fast-track they will need to work together as a group from Year 9, which has implications for grouping across the whole of the Year 9 cohort. Overall, fast-tracking by cohorts of pupils seems to have little to offer in most subjects and even in mathematics may be of questionable value.

For individuals the idea of fast-tracking may be more appropriate. In theory individual pupils could work with older pupils for some parts of the timetable without a great deal of disruption. Indeed this already happens in some schools where individual circumstances dictate such an approach. At present however, the number of pupils who could be accommodated in this way is limited. A detailed programme is required for each child to ensure that they continue to receive their curriculum entitlement, as outlined in the National Curriculum. If working with an older group for maths means a child missing his or her class PE lesson then this PE time must be made up elsewhere. Significant numbers of students working with older pupils in a variety of subjects would lead to a logistical nightmare.

In considering fast-tracking for individuals, schools should perhaps be looking to the future rather than making a 'knee-jerk' response to individual circumstances. In which subjects is fast-tracking likely to be of value and should these departments be reassessing their provision with this in mind? Modern foreign languages is an interesting arena for a fast-tracking debate. The number of pupils who are bilingual in European languages is increasing, with families working abroad and as a result of extra-curricular French teaching. How should a department respond to its pupils arriving in Year 7 already achieving a range of levels in French?

Streaming

This is another option which is often suggested as a way of ensuring that the needs of able pupils are met. This means selecting pupils on the basis of their all-round ability and educating them as a group or stream. This is one way to ensure appropriate pace but has major drawbacks in that many very able pupils do not have all-round ability. Most streaming is based on verbal reasoning and those with abilities in other areas may not make the top stream. This is a system with some advantages but it is also very inflexible and fails to recognize the links between ability and achievement.

Setting

This is grouping on a subject-by-subject basis. It is better suited to ensuring that all those with ability are given appropriate opportunities. There are some problems here with the selection for top sets being based on present achievement rather than potential, but overall there are fewer problems than with other systems. Setting is generally very good for those in the top set but has demotivating effects on others and so is not used in all subjects throughout all schools. Some subjects seem to be more easily taught in sets. Regardless of how early or frequently a school sets, mathematics is usually the first subject to be set, followed by modern foreign languages. English often remains in mixed-ability groupings until Year 9 and sometimes until Year 11. Able pupils, when interviewed, usually express a preference for setted classes where the pace is often faster and they are free to achieve without fear of ridicule.

Mixed-ability teaching

Some very good teachers can successfully extend their most able within a mixed-ability context. It takes careful planning and monitoring, but it can be done. It is, however, very demanding and whilst teachers often say that it is the fairest system, poor mixed-ability teaching is deadly for able pupils. They are demotivated by a slow pace and inhibited from doing well by adverse comments from other pupils. Teachers often rely on their most able to get on alone so that they have time to deal with others. Able pupils get very little teacher time in poorly taught, mixed-ability lessons and underachievement often occurs.

Well differentiated mixed-ability lessons can be successful, but planned differentiation for the most able is not a regular feature of lessons in many schools. When considering the use of mixed-ability teaching it is helpful to look at the possible as well as the desirable. Often the head of department who is a strong advocate of mixed-ability teaching is also an excellent teacher. She or he may not appreciate that others in the department do not have quite such advanced skills. *If mixed-ability teaching is to be the adopted methodology within a department for all or some years, then differentiation must be a departmental priority.*

Able pupils must not be allowed to underachieve simply because the system is seen as the fairest for most pupils. Able pupils must be subject to high expectations and carefully monitored to ensure that they are achieving at an appropriate level.

Whole-school opportunities

Schools generally offer a wide range of opportunities that fall outside normal classroom provision. Such opportunities are often highly influential in the schooling of able pupils and can in some cases be of greater significance than actual lessons. With the pressure of the National Curriculum and examinations, these opportunities can sometimes be overlooked. From a management perspective, they can encourage excellence and at the same time provide a showcase for parents. From the pupil's point of view, they allow time and opportunity to work in depth, be it on theatrical lighting or on Latin.

Many schools underestimate the number of whole-school opportunities that are available to students. Drawing up a list provides some surprising insights – for example the modern languages department which did not think it provided any additional opportunities but takes three separate groups to France each year, etc. This is to some extent a question of perception. For this department the commitment was so regular it no longer seemed like an addition. In tackling provision for able pupils, a school needs to look carefully at both what is provided within lesson time and also what is extra-curricular. Especially in the early years of the secondary school, class lessons offer few opportunities for pupils to work in depth on a specific subject whereas extra-curricular activities can offer this opportunity in a relaxed and sociable environment. The types of whole-school activities most schools offer to enrich and extend their pupils fall into ten broad categories (see Figure 5.3).

Roles and responsibilities

From the management perspective, allocating responsibility for elements of the school's provision is crucial to its success. Good provision is integral to the life of the school but for this to occur key players have to undertake their part. In the early days of school interest in able pupils, responsibility was often given as an allowance post to an individual coordinator and she or he was expected to tackle the issue largely alone. This person was frequently quite lowly in the management structure and was often unable to influence departmental decisions and attitudes. The outcome was an approach focused on extra-curricular enrichment activities for able pupils since these were the only opportunities the coordinator could facilitate personally. Whilst such activities are very useful, they are essentially an 'extra' and do not have an impact on departmental activity, so in these early examples departmental provision often remained unchanged.

It is now well recognized that provision must be part of the designated responsibility of a range of personnel, including at least one member of the senior management team. The senior management team will give the work status and their interest will ensure that it is addressed by all relevant colleagues. They are in a strong position to facilitate work and have a unique opportunity to maintain an overview of activity. Figure 5.4 shows the range of staff who need to take some responsibility for the school's provision for able children, and the nature of those responsibilities.

Examples of activities provided at whole-school level for More Able Pupils

1. **Withdrawal groups**
   Activities organized by subject departments, e.g. Year 8 maths extension group; 'able writers' – Years 7, 8 and 9.

2. **Enrichment days**
   Able pupils freed from timetable constraints to focus on cross-curricular challenges. (Some schools release all pupils from the timetable to offer enrichment activities but create particular opportunities for able pupils.)

3. **Residentials**
   Weekends run either by learning support departments or by subject departments. Selected pupils invited to attend, e.g. Warwick past and present – Years 7, 8 and 9, maths weekend – Years 8 and 9, modern languages weekend.

4. **Off-site opportunities**
   Buying into commercially-run opportunities to provide extension for individuals or groups of pupils, e.g. 'talented young writers', industry days; GIFT activities.

5. **After-school clubs**
   Open to all pupils but some types may be particularly appealing to pupils with specific abilities or talents, e.g. cricket club, yoga, Latin club, technology club.

6. **Extra clubs**
   Clubs established to provide for 'academic' pupils in Years 7 and 8. Tutor support provided to facilitate the development of personal interest projects.

7. **Competitions**
   Pupils with particular abilities encouraged to take part in school, local or national competitions, e.g. Year 9 chemistry competition; maths challenge – senior (6th form), intermediate (Years 9 and 10), junior (Years 7 and 8).

8. **Whole-school opportunities**
   Ensuring able pupils take advantage of the wide range of whole-school opportunities, e.g. drama productions, musical events, visits abroad, work placements.

9. **Accredited courses**
   Able pupils using the Youth Award Scheme in Year 8 to accredit community and other projects. Sixth formers working on Open University modules in maths.

10. **Staff working groups**
    Many schools have a working group of staff, which meets regularly to consider whole-school and departmental provision for able pupils, e.g. children to challenge group. Some such groups are allocated time or finance to fund particular projects.

Figure 5.3 Examples of whole-school activity

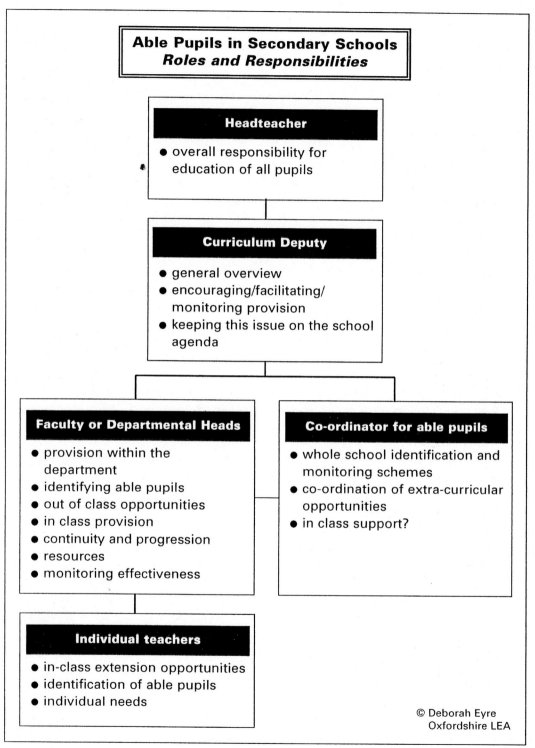

Figure 5.4 Roles and responsibilities in the secondary school

The coordinator for able pupils

The coordinator for able pupils needs to be an enthusiast. She or he must be capable of encouraging and supporting other staff and of keeping the needs of able pupils on the school agenda. The coordinator also needs to be reliable and systematic, as they will have the major role in creating and monitoring the effectiveness of identification systems. As with all co-ordinating roles, good interpersonal skills are crucial if others in the school are to be cajoled, and sometimes pressed, into improving departmental provision. It is these characteristics that seem to determine the effectiveness of the coordinator's role, rather than its location within the school structure. Therefore in seeking a suitable coordinator, personality should be more important than his or her other roles within the school.

Structurally, the coordinator is most frequently located within the special needs or learning support department. This is consistent with the idea that such a department should be responsible for the individual needs of a variety of pupils. Indeed such departments are sometimes called the 'individual needs department'. There are some disadvantages in locating the able pupil coordinator post in this department, primarily related to time and priority although they can sometimes also be linked to approach. An SEN department has a wide range of legal and other responsibilities for pupils covered under the *Code of Practice on the Identification and Assessment of Special Educational Needs* (DfEE, 1994); as a result, time available to devote to provision for able pupils may be limited. The *Code of Practice* is set within the legal framework of the 1993 Education Act and therefore must be implemented. Able pupil provision falls into the 'guidance' category and is not legally binding in the same way. In addition, some staff within the department may see the needs of able pupils as a less pressing educational issue than the needs of SEN pupils. If the school's provision for able pupils is to be effective, the able pupil coordinator must be the school's engine for action and so must not be located in a part of the school where it will be given low priority.

Another possible difficulty in respect of SEN departments may be in the approach used. The able pupil coordinator should not become responsible for all the pupils identified as able, since the case-load would be enormous. Responsibility must stay primarily with the heads of department. It may be that the school decides to create a 'case-load' group comprising pupils who are recognized as able in five or six areas of the curriculum, or where pupils have outstanding ability (nominally the top 2 per cent) but this is not a key component of effective provision. It simply facilitates the monitoring of provision by creating a clearly identified group to focus upon. In some instances this difference in approach between provision for the most able and SEN provision can cause problems. The SEN department may be used to working with clearly identified pupils and subject departments may also expect this approach from the SEN department. The creation of a 'case-load' or 'focus' group can exacerbate this problem as it leads to an assumption, on the part of both SEN and subject departments, that all the school's able pupils are in this group. In fact only good all-rounders are in the focus group; pupils with outstanding aptitudes and talents in a more limited range of domains will not feature.

The above considerations do not mean that locating the able coordinator in the SEN department is impossible, only that it needs to be handled carefully. Three of the best co-ordinators I have met have been in SEN departments; however, they are usually responsible only for the most able, even if a part of their timetable includes other SEN work.

Other successful coordinators have been heads of other departments. Heads of English, maths and science have all been successful. The advantage of locating the coordinator role within a subject is that it encourages a curriculum-focused response. This may facilitate more effective progress on differentiation issues. Able pupil coordinators based in subject departments tend to be most interested in developing departmental provision. They usually start by focusing on their own department and then use this experience as the basis of development work in other departments. This kind of approach carries authority and is likely to lead to significant progress. However, subject-based coordinators are likely to have less expertise in the monitoring of individuals and this may have to be done elsewhere.

It is difficult to be definitive regarding the optimum structural location for a coordinator for able pupils. A school where the coordinator is within a department is likely to make rapid progress in departmental provision. Where the coordinator is within the SEN department, progress is likely to be best in the identification and monitoring of individuals. A possible consideration is a change of location when one particular aspect of provision is well established; this may help to move the emphasis to another area.

Clearly the remit of the coordinator will vary, depending upon his or her other roles within the school. She or he should, however, be primarily responsible for coordinating departmental provision and identification and monitoring schemes. In addition, she or he should encourage the establishment of appropriate curricular enhancement opportunities as well as a range of extra-curricular opportunities. Below is an example of how one coordinator, Susan Macmillan, interprets her role.

The Programme for More Able Children at The Henry Box School

I am a teacher in the Learning Support Department at the Henry Box School and I receive an allowance to develop and coordinate an enrichment programme for our more able students. The Learning Support Department aims to encourage and provide educational opportunities over and above those supplied during the normal school timetable, since the ablest pupils are regarded as a set of children who have special educational needs.

The school aims to develop the potential of all pupils and the main forum for the education of our most able pupils continues to be in mainstream classroom lessons. Subject departments make special provision for pupils of higher ability. This involves a number of approaches such as setting, differentiation by resources and teaching techniques, field courses, etc. For example, as part of the normal curriculum the Art Department regularly arranges for an 'Artist in Residence' to work with the particularly able artists, the Mathematics Department invites target pupils to take part in the 'Maths Challenge', and the English Department withdraws target pupils to work on extension materials and projects. One of the most exciting developments of coordinating this programme has been to pass on the baton to departments who have taken it over and are now 'running with it'.

The enrichment programme is mainly in-house provision, relying on the enthusiasm and expertise of the teaching staff. For the past four years I have chaired a support group composed of members of each subject department. Meeting once a term, teaching staff pool ideas for activities which are then coordinated into a 'balanced' enrichment programme. The aim is to provide one activity session for most able students in Years 7 to 9, each term. The programme is published at the beginning of the academic year and the participating pupils receive a copy of the timetable with their invitation to participate in the first enrichment session.

An activity session is in addition to the normal timetable subjects. Its purpose is to provide extension work for those who it is felt would benefit from it. Pupils are under no compulsion to attend. The sessions aim to pose intellectual challenge for the pupils based on quality rather than quantity of work. The activities provide opportunities for originality and imagination through problem solving and creativity and self-direction through thought and action. For example, this year's programme has included an introduction to the Greek alphabet (Year 7), English Language work based on Shakespeare's *Julius Caesar* (Year 8) and participation in a Science Fair (Year 9).

The identification of our most able students continues to be a rigorous and continuous process. I compile a register of the most able students based on primary school information, SATs scores at Key Stages 2 and 3 and monitoring and school reporting procedures. Recently a new Review Card System has been introduced and this has proved particularly useful in identifying the underachieving but able students. In January I carried out a research project into the accuracy of our record keeping and whether we had correctly identified all our most able students. Using GCSE results from 1995, I awarded points for grades of C and above and cross-referenced the sum of these scores with the names of the students on the Able Pupils Register. Only one student had not been identified as a more able student and had not participated in the enrichment programme. From my research it appears that teacher recommendation is the most accurate predictor of student ability and subsequent achievement in examinations!

On completion of each part of the programme, students are required to log their personal response to their studies and performance. This gives the student an opportunity for self-assessment in order to develop higher order thinking skills and a chance to set individual targets to develop quality and depth of work and understanding. These responses are monitored and certain pupils are then tracked in some subjects by a member of the Learning Support Department.

Ongoing research into the 'value' of the programme has produced some interesting results. Most students in Years 11 and 12 can remember activity sessions in detail and give positive responses to my questionnaires. Some of the most memorable comments include those of Abbi:

> I was surprised to be told that I had potential. My mum worked in the Co-op to bring me and my brother up. I had no ambitions at all. You told us that we would be the managers of the future and that we owed it to ourselves and society to make the most of ourselves.

Abbi is now an area manager of a large pharmaceutical company. Emily gained her Private Pilots Licence at the age of eighteen having won an RAF scholarship. She had taken part in an enrichment course which we called 'Flight', based on a Royal

Institution Masterclass conducted by Sir Christopher Zeeman, one of the world's leading mathematicians. Graham has recently gained an upper second in Geology. He told me he was inspired to take this subject after participating in a residential course, The Geology of the Universe.

The delivery of the programme would be made more efficient if sessions could be timetabled in advance and published in the school diary. This could be possible next year. Also, I would like to run more cross-curricular rather than subject-based sessions and thereby forge inter-departmental collaboration. Members of the Art and Science departments are already collaborating in the development of enrichment programmes. Their latest initiative has been to use the Karl André exhibition at our local museum of modern art, to develop the skills of abler pupils in maths and science, by looking at how the structure of materials can influence creative ideas. We are fortunate to have a classics scholar on the staff who has been a main contributor to the programme, developing classical and historically-based activities.

I hope that with the continued enthusiasm and commitment from the teaching staff and other expert volunteers the programme for our most able students will continue to encourage and inspire many pupils to make the most of their educational opportunities at The Henry Box School.

Susan Macmillan

Faculty or subject departments

Provision for able pupils will not be effective unless *most* staff within the school are involved. Almost all of a pupil's learning experiences take place in lessons or activities created by subject departments, and hence so too should the opportunities for challenge. The main responsibilities for a department include the provision of challenging opportunities on a day-to-day basis in the classroom, curriculum enhancement opportunities and monitoring of the progress of individuals.

A department needs to consider whether its organizational structures really do facilitate good provision. There is much rhetoric regarding the advantages and/or disadvantages of setting, fast-tracking, etc. In reality the questions to consider are:

What constitutes the best provision for able pupils?

Which can be created without jeopardizing the education of others?

Is it really possible to provide for able children in a mixed-ability context?

Does too much setting restrict opportunities for some youngsters?

One way to find out if the present arrangements work is to ask the pupils, in this case the most able. They will quickly and eloquently provide an overview of their present experiences.

Provision includes both that which is included in ordinary lessons and that which is provided by departments in addition. Some additional provision is provided for all pupils, e.g. French trips or geography field trips, and some is targeted specifically at those who have marked aptitude or ability. Figure 5.5 is a list from a typical comprehensive school which sees provision of a wide range of opportunities as an essential part of its able pupil provision.

Curriculum enhancement
- Toastmaster International Workshops in Year 10
- Extending research facilities in the Library (including the Internet, satellite TV, CD-ROMS and a bar-coded database) – all years
- Offering Reading Awards – Years 7 and 8
- Setting up a student bookshop – all years
- Having a 'Boys and Reading' week – all years
- Introducing the Duke of Edinburgh Award Scheme through Mrs. Valerie Probert – Years 9–13
- Beginners' Latin –Year 9
- Writing for the 'Schools Mail' – Year 10
- French and German Exchanges – Years 9 and 10
- Debates – all years
- Public speaking – Years 9 and 10
- Maths Challenge – Years 8 and 9
- Work Experience for all in Year 10 / some Year 12
- Theatre in Education in school – Year 10
- Residential Maths course in Southampton – Years 12 and 13
- Visits to the Science Museum – Years 10 and 11
- Visits to art galleries – Years 12 and 13
- A Sixth Form Conference
- Geographical field trip – Years 7/8/10/12/13
- History trip – Year 7
- Preparing a time capsule for the *Oxford Mail* – Year 8
- Extending our mini-network into Maths Department (complementing Busines Studies, Technology, Geography, History, Languages and Science) – all years
- Science Master Class – Year 10
- After-school study club in the Library – all years

Extra-curricular events
- Business Challenge – Year 11
- Sailing Club – all years
- Theatre trips – Years 10–13
- Concerts – all years
- A superb production of *A Midsummer Night's Dream* over three nights – all years
- An outdoor experience in Glasbury – Year 9
- A week's induction in Year 12
- A half-term holiday in Barcelona – Years 12 and 13
- A skiing holiday – Years 9–13
- Success in many sporting areas, including athletics, soccer, rugby – all years
- Rover Skills Club on Saturdays – Year 11
- Model United Nations General Assembly – Year 12
- Saturday Challenge Day – Years 8 and 9

Figure 5.5 Activities at Matthew Arnold School

A crucial aspect of departmental provision is the creation of effective continuity and progression. It is only by having a clear picture of the developmental continuum that individual teachers will be able to assess pupil progress. Able pupils are frequently held back by lack of diagnostic assessment. A typical knowledge and conceptual level for each age group is assumed and planning based upon this. Able pupils could often go further but teachers perceive a difficulty based on the invasion into next year's work. If the department's work is seen as continuous and seamless rather than linked to certain years, then it is easier to allow pupils to progress at an appropriate rate.

Good target setting and monitoring schemes are also important in ensuring good provision. Pupil achievement can be raised substantially by helping pupils to recognize personal targets, and monitoring, with them, their progress against the targets set. This is true for all students but is particularly true for able pupils whose personal targets may exceed those being set for the class generally. For pupils who are habitually top of the class it is important to ensure that progress made is appropriate to their ability level and not just judged against general class expectations.

Individual teachers make a difference

Although much of a secondary school's approach to able pupils is determined at middle or senior management level, individual teachers can make a significant impact on provision. It is of course individual teachers who either make the school's approach work or neutralize it, but they can also be proactive in making changes both in their own classroom and in their department. Sometimes it is a young teacher coming into school with new ideas who helps a department recognize greater possibilities. Sometimes it is a teacher who has already become highly proficient at delivering the regular curriculum and who is looking for greater professional challenge.

Case Study. Susan Blake, Didcot Girls School, Oxfordshire.

Susan Blake was already an experienced English teacher when she began to experiment with ways to create greater challenge in the English curriculum. She outlines her general approach as follows.

Some approaches used to create challenge for more able pupils in English
Years 7-13

1. Different learning aims
Core – to develop a more confident awareness of different styles employed by authors to describe childhood experience
Ext. – to develop a more sophisticated descriptive style by using metaphor

2. Different short term aims
Core – to add descriptions of expressions, movements to a description of a character
to create character by creating their thoughts and reactions
to create character using a stream of consciousness

3. Different models of writing and different expectation of readers
Core – a direct, factual text, e.g. charity leaflet focus on layout and language
Ext. – two sets of information about historic places for critical evaluation and comparison

4. Different texts
Core – different poems on the same theme e.g. love
Ext. – different prose extracts with widely different styles, views and cultural background

5. Different challenges within core task
Core – one pupil organising four pieces of information about a castle for visitors
Ext. – one pair moving away from leaflet format to attract visitors
Ext. – one pupil persuading visitors to an alternative site focusing on a particular audience, e.g. young children

6. Different types of presentation requiring different oral or written skills and styles
Core – one pupil persuading class to go to invented stately home
Ext. – one pupil giving critical account of decisions taken and process followed during the work on an informative guide

7. Different tasks with different written outcomes: requiring different routes through work, different styles and different strengths in writer
Core – one pupil writing a personal statement about involvement in a fictitious crime
Ext. – one pupil conducting a police investigation/news interview

8. Different work partnerships: roles within groups
Core – grouping pupils working on the same aim or similar style of writing pairing pupils who have different strengths or different approaches to writing
Ext. – varying the roles of pupils within a group to foster new skills encouraging critical dialogue between pairs or groups to encourage peer support

9. Different work processes
Core – one group listing simple initial ideas for collaborative writing task one group carrying out information research with specific questions
Ext. – one group conducting own research with independently chosen research topic

10. Different investigation questions
Core – one pair considering what role a character plays in a scene, e.g. Ophelia one pair considering the dramatic techniques employed in a scene by the playwright
Ext. – one group considering decisions made by poet/playwright about character, plot, scene, choice of language, imagery, choice of form/structure: explaining decisions in role of poet/playwright

11. Different types of reading
Core – one pupil focusing on simple details in narrative build up of a scene or

aspect of the plot
one pupil focusing on central character and what is established about her/him
one pupil developing awareness of the clues laid by the author about the fate of a character or the outcome of an event
Ext. –   one pupil comparing two authors' styles, or novel openings, or use of narrative style, authorial voice or narrative manipulation, etc.

12. Different ways of recording information and ideas
Core - sketches, speech bubbles, stick people, logs, character-diaries, graphs, Venn diagrams, shopping lists, story-boards, auto-cue scripts

13. Different homework tasks
Core – one group writing a poison pen letter
one group composing a speech to give in a role-play trial taking the role of key character
Ext. –   one group writing in style of author from an alternative point of view

She has developed a range of fascinating units to encourage pupils to strive for excellence rather than being content with the acceptable. The example in Figure 5.6 comes from Year 9 (14 years). Susan Blake describes this Year 9 group as of mixed ability, with ten able students and three extremely talented. She also describes them as being decidedly 'unkeen' on extending their expertise or trying anything different. Figure 5.6 shows the worksheet for the extension group and their instructions. This unit is undertaken by all pupils but the level of demand is increased in the extension sheet.

Susan describes the outcome thus:

They feed me ideas, and make suggestions about adapting tasks to increase the challenge. The Green Radio task became a Green TV task for one group who felt that writing for TV would be tougher than a radio broadcast. They also wanted to move away from a fixed script and buckets of notes drawn from traditional research. They were determined not to lift chunks of text from other sources. We worked on a system of recording snippets of information on dictaphones rather than 40 pages of neatly written research notes. They designed a home-made auto-cue that had only prompt points on it. This was then used as a prompt when the video was filmed to guide their improvised speeches. The group learnt only the key ideas that needed to be communicated to the audience and worked these into their statements.

Melanie, one of the pupils involved, wrote in her review sheet:

Despite there being four of us with individual jobs, we all seemed to help each other. We used the school and public libraries and rang charities that we felt could give us relevant information. At the beginning we seemed to be striving for more facts and figures but in the end we seemed to be overflowing with information. I was the writer and found I used my writing skills to good effect but I found it hard to organise all the notes we had made. It was quite annoying when we had pieces of writing that just wouldn't flow together but the editor used her skills to alter the writing slightly but still keep the depth and detail of

Green Radio 109.9 F.M.

Your Task

To research, write, script, rehearse and broadcast a short radio programme (10 minutes) about environmental issues on a Green Radio Chanel 109 FM

Where to start

You could broadcast for 24 hours there are so many environmental issues causing interest, or concern. Before you begin agree on a format for your programme e.g. one issue considered in a debate style from both sides, or a range of stories of different lengths.

What is the aim of your broadcast

Do you want listeners to
Become active protesters, or join a national environmental group, e.g. Friends of the Earth, or get out into local environment to help with conservation work, or become more green aware, use of resources more carefully and recycle, or entertain young and teenage listeners so that they join in with environmental movement, or feel shocked into action?, or your own aim?

Selection of programme material

Selecting some issues from such a huge range will be tricky. It will help if you stick with one theme, e.g. The Ocean, or one issue, e.g. Pollution.

Organisation

It will make your work much more manageable if people in the group know what they are responsible for, and what they have to do.

Decide who is going to do what! You will need: research asistants, writers, an editor, one or two presenters.

Complete the group responsibility chart overleaf. Plan out the work you will need to do so that you can complete your particular job.

The programme will be a combination of everyone's work.

Figure 5.6 Extension work sheet

Stage One

What style of programme will help you to meet your aim?
e.g. a combination of music and reports, or interviews and information bulletins

What type of information will you need to meet your aim?

What do you need to find out before you can get writing? Jot down as many questions as possible

Where will you find this information, e.g. library, CD ROM, text books, Green Peace

Stage Two

Researchers visit libraries, contact with relevant organisations: if you request written material check how long it may take to arrive. Use questionnaires and dictaphones for interviews.

Writers begin drafting stories/articles/interviews etc. as soon as you have any details

Stage Three

Editor get into action. Work on:
Length of stories
Amount of detail in each sentence and paragraph
Style of language
Fluency of story from start to finish
Impact of story
Finally: Order of stories for broadcast: which story would make the best lead, or round-off?

Stage Four

Presenters rehearse with direction and support from team

Stage Five

Record broadcast with all material, additional input, e.g. relevant records, interviews, headlines

Broadcast to Year Seven on Green Radio 109.9 F.M.

the pieces. My only hope is that the listening audience try and learn something and even get a bit upset about what we have said so that these charities can gain support from them.

I've enjoyed this project a lot and we all seemed to work well together – even when it wasn't working. We offered each other support and constructive criticism which helped us polish everything off. The work has given us a platform to work on and an insight into media work and trying to meet deadlines. We can go on to build on our knowledge and next time it will be even better.

Clearly Susan Blake's approach to extending the most able is carefully considered, well planned and provides continuity as pupils progress from Years 7 to 13. Extension planning is fully integrated into her way of working and pupils meet tasks of different types to develop different strengths. Of course this kind of approach requires a thorough knowledge of the pupils being taught. A different approach may be needed in a subject where the teacher meets the pupils less frequently. However, if provision is to be effective each teacher and subject department needs to consider the ways best suited to their situation.

Summary

In order for a secondary school to make effective provision for its most able pupils it must consider a wide range of issues at classroom, departmental and senior management level. Schools which have good provision have clearly defined aims in respect of their most able and set up organizational systems that facilitate these aims. A large number of personnel will be involved in delivering and monitoring provision and extension will be a regular feature of classroom activity.

Schools which are successful in creating appropriate opportunities reach a stage where provision is so well integrated into the school that it becomes difficult to identify all its different forms. However, a good coordinator sees the monitoring of opportunities as a feature of his or her role combined with the monitoring of pupils.

Schools working towards establishing effective provision may find Figure 5.7 a useful *aide-mémoire.*

A Comprehensive Response to High Ability Pupils in Secondary Schools

1. Identification and Monitoring

- Pupils identified on a 'subject-specific' basis and details made available to all Staff.
- Performance then monitored on a regular basis for early identification of any problem areas.

2. Out of Class Activities

- Opportunities for able pupils to work together. This may include cross-year as well as cross-class work.
- Interest-led activities provided by faculties or departments. These often take the form of short residentials or timetable-free days.

3. School Organisation and Structure

- A school structure which recognises and accommodates the needs of high ability pupils. This may include opportunities for an exceptional child to work with an older class for some lessons.
- Organisation that meets the needs of all pupils, including the most able. This may include setting but could equally well be mixed-ability based, if carefully administered.
- Recognition of achievements, in a broad framework.

4. Class-based Learning

- Real challenge on a day to day basis in the classroom. Opportunities that encourage pupils to work at higher cognitive levels.
- Flexibility of teaching styles to allow for real differentiation, even within setted classes.
- Appropriate, probably differentiated homework.

5. Personal and Social

- A recognition that self-esteem and high attainment are closely linked and that highly able pupils have need of personal and social education.
- Systems that allow for close links between parents and school. High ability, like learning difficulties, may need parents and school to work together closely to effect an appropriate educational response.

Deborah Eyre,
Oxfordshire LEA

Figure 5.7 A comprehensive approach

Chapter 6

Issues for Primary Schools

Introduction

As with secondary schools, a lack of challenge is a common 'key issue' in OFSTED reports on primary schools. Some primary schools have given very little consideration to the needs of their most able children either because they do not perceive themselves to have any or in the mistaken belief that able children will 'get on anyway' and do not need particular consideration. Even in schools where a policy for able children exists, either separately or as part of an SEN policy, a lack of challenge may still be an identified issue. This of course illustrates a gap between policy and practice. Whilst teachers may recognize what able children need, it is not always a normal aspect of their classroom provision. One problem here is talking about able children as a clearly defined group. Many teachers will agree on what needs to be done for such children, but do not recognize that they have any in their class. OFSTED inspectors however are looking at each lesson from the perspective of children who could go further in that lesson. When they use the term 'most able', it is in relation to the lesson they have seen. Therefore the most able in the English lesson may be different from the most able in the art lesson, for example.

This chapter explores the role of headteachers, governors and teachers in ensuring that the most able are challenged in all aspects of the curriculum and in all year groups. It supplements the chapters on identification and differentiation, and it examines in more detail issues specifically related to primary school management and class-teaching. It offers practical strategies for headteachers and identifies issues which may need consideration. For the class teacher it offers guidance on some of the management issues which influence effective implementation of extension planning.

The management of provision for able children in the primary school is by no means easy. This is amply demonstrated by the number of schools which have recognized the need to provide for able children, and may even have gone so far as to identify them within the school, yet still find this appearing as a key issue in OFSTED inspection reports. The main difficulty is related to the fact that good provision has implications for a variety of school structures and systems. Coming new to this area of work it would be easy to assume that good provision simply involves identifying able children and ensuring that an individual programme of work is provided for them. In reality this approach is both frustrating and ineffective. *A school will not be effective in its provision for able children if it limits itself to the identification of able individuals and individual programmes of work for them.* The meeting of individual needs, whilst valid, is only part of a much bigger picture (see Figure 6.1).

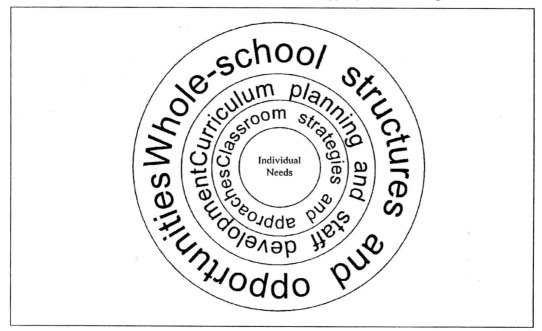

Figure 6.1 Circles

Establishing good provision is a medium- to long-term development issue; it requires careful planning and target setting and is best tackled under the headings advocated by the school improvement literature: (OFSTED, 1994)

- Taking stock and auditing present provision
- Making the plan
- Implementing the plan
- Evaluating the outcomes.

Commitment

Crucial to the effectiveness of any area of work are the shared values and commitment of all the school staff. This is particularly important in development work for able pupils because there is considerable chance of misunderstandings about motives and appropriateness. In the minds of some teachers there still lingers a concern about elitism and a suspicion that education for able children may be at the expense of other children. In reality the reverse is true. *Considering the needs of able children should be part of ensuring the entitlement of all children to an appropriate education.* Therefore, one could say that appropriate provision is a part of offering equality of opportunity. Tim Brighouse (Chief Education Officer, Birmingham) has made the useful point that equality of opportunity should mean diversity rather than sameness: different provision for different children, not the same for all. Many staff fears are allayed if the school adopts a wide definition of ability and recognizes that significant numbers of children may have ability in one subject or in a limited range of areas (see Chapter 1). Immediately, work on able children becomes more generally relevant and an important aspect of the work of all teachers.

There also needs to be discussion at this point regarding the kind of provision the school should make. Once again it is likely that there will be a range of responses to this. Some will be strongly attracted to setting or ability grouping, others will stress the need for mixed-ability opportunities. A more helpful discussion might be concerned with what the school should be trying to provide for its most able children rather than a discussion of organizational structures. Most schools agree that their provision for able children should include both extension (take subjects into greater depth) and enrichment (adding breadth to the curriculum). *Enriching and Extending the National Curriculum* (Eyre and Marjoram, 1990) explores this issue and looks at how a school can combine enrichment and extension to create a challenging curriculum.

The whole question of how best to educate the most able is worthy of extensive discussion because it allows staff to develop a greater understanding of the broad issues, so enabling them to speak more effectively to parents. Most teachers instinctively recognize that moving swiftly through a narrow range of content or concepts is less effective than combining it with chances to use and apply this knowledge. However, without a proper consideration of the issues this explanation can be presented to parents in a less than convincing manner. To give an example: a teacher said,

> We recognize that your child is intellectually very able but he isn't very good at mixing with other children. So we have decided to concentrate on his social skills.

This kind of response can leave a parent feeling that intellectual capacity is undervalued; that the school is addressing a perceived deficit but ignoring the talent. One reason for such comments lies in teacher confidence. Whilst most teachers can easily explain their overall approach to reading or to behaviour problems, a summary of their approach to extending able children can be less clearly articulated. Most teachers are able to decide on strategies to overcome any social problems; the route forward intellectually may be less clear.

In general terms the school might take a stance along the following lines:

> *When children are learning new ideas or concepts, we are looking for them to become familiar with the concept, demonstrate their understanding of the concept by using it, and then demonstrate that they have added the concept to their repertoire by applying that concept in a variety of other areas.*

Application is particularly significant in the education of the most able. For many children that final stage is the one which causes the difficulty: children can do the page of sums but may not be able to tackle maths problems which need the same skills, to learn about one period in History but not recognize the similarities between periods. Application is sometimes described as an ability to see the big picture. It is something which comes naturally to able pupils and needs encouragement and nurture.

How can a school encapsulate its approach to the most able? Should this be expressly explained to all parents before their children start school? If a school is to be effective in its provision for able children then the approach used should be clearly understood by staff, governors and parents.

Policy

The school's policy must not be a sterile document, created at a staff meeting and lodged in the filing cabinet ever since, but rather a working document subject to change and review. An able children policy, as with all policy, can be created by using the top-down or bottom-up approach. In a top-down model, the policy is created based on what provision should be like and includes areas for the school to develop; these are then transferred to other development documents for action and time-scales. The alternative model starts from recording what presently exists within the school and is subject to regular updating.

In either instance certain principles hold. The policy will only be accepted and be a true reflection of what happens in school if all staff really agree with what is decided and are prepared to make changes. In practice many teachers, faced with a range of new initiatives and ideas, stop challenging each one at whole-school level and instead simply fail to implement the agreed changes in their classroom. This leads not only to uneven provision but also to progression problems in school.

In the case of able children, staff need to agree on definitions to be used, systems for identification and recognition, the approach to classroom planning and activities outside of class which supplement classroom provision. Appendix 1 provides a framework to assist schools in policy making. Appendix 2 is an example of such a policy from an Oxford middle school.

Sharing this policy with governors and parents is essential to its success. Many people, when they first consider provision for able children, do expect that the school will be moving children up to higher classes, introducing extensive setting or ability grouping and, in short, reinventing a selective system. If your school approach is to be a blend of enrichment and extension then it will be necessary to explain why such an approach has been adopted and how it works in practice. Why, for example, is there value in providing a range of opportunities to 'use and apply' information, instead of quickly moving on to the next set of concepts?

Staff responsibilities for able pupil provision

Ultimately it is of course the responsibility of the headteacher and the governors to ensure appropriate challenge for the most able. This means that the school's management team must be clear in their own minds about the indicators of effective provision. Unfortunately, whilst appropriate guidance for SEN is clearly documented in the *Code of Practice on the Identification and Assessment of Special Educational Needs* (DfEE, 1994), little government guidance exists on provision for the most able. Therefore headteachers may not be entirely conversant with the elements of good provision. This issue is compounded by a lack of inservice training available for heads, teachers, or governors. Fortunately some LEAs now provide guidance in the form of a policy document. These often provide a very useful analysis of the main issues coupled with ideas and strategies. In addition, the DfEE in conjunction with NACE has produced a booklet for school governors, outlining the main issues, entitled *School Governors and More Able Children* (Eyre, 1996).

Responsibility for implementation of school policy may vary according to the size and nature of the school. Holyport CE Primary School (Berkshire) has a coordinator for able pupils. St Anne's CEVC School (Bristol) makes provision an aspect of all curriculum coordinators' roles. In many of Oxfordshire's small schools the headteacher takes on this responsibility as part of his or her role. Different models can be equally effective provided that their implementation is carefully considered.

Able child coordinator

One way of working is for a named person to have responsibility for able child provision. This has specific advantages. It ensures that the needs of the most able are consistently part of the school's agenda. Whenever a subject area is being discussed, the coordinator will ask about the implications for the most able in that subject. She or he may keep a register of those identified as more able and review their progress with individual staff. Also, she or he may be responsible for the purchase of generic resources. The major disadvantages of this approach centre around finance and ownership. First, such a post is likely to need financial recognition, usually in the form of an allowance post. This may be considered too great an expense for the school budget, although large primary schools should look carefully at the possibility. Second, if one member of staff has responsibility for the most able, other staff may feel they no longer have to concern themselves with this issue. The school may find this leads to a heavy emphasis on withdrawal activities for able children and little regular extension in the classroom.

Careful use of a coordinator post can bring immense benefits to a school but it does need careful planning and monitoring. The job description for the Holyport School has developed over a number of years and describes the way is which the coordinator interacts with other staff to ensure a whole-school approach:

Holyport CE Primary School

ABLE CHILD COORDINATOR

1. To monitor the Able Child Policy for the school.

2. To maintain a register of all able children in the school following consultation with the teaching and support staff and, where appropriate, to liaise with parents.

3. To develop, in conjunction with the class teacher, an Individual Education Plan for children as and when required.

4. To help staff with their short-term planning to ensure a differentiated curriculum.

5. To keep staff informed of current thinking in the field of able children and to give advice when necessary.

6. To attend any relevant courses on able children.

7. To liaise with the Inset coordinator on staff needs for In-Service in relation to able children.

8. To analyse, with the Headteacher, the annual NFER tests, the BPVS and the Nebraska Protocol results.

9. To purchase and organize resources for able children within the school budget.

A different approach shares the responsibility across a number of people in the school. Each curriculum coordinator is responsible for more able provision in his or her subject, and year leaders for provision for their year or sector of the school. This approach has the advantage of permeating the whole structure of the school. Everyone is responsible for the most able. In theory this should be the more effective method but in practice it needs the headteacher to take a very active monitoring role to be successful. If everyone has a little responsibility then it is easy for the focus to become blurred or lost: everyone yet no one holds the ultimate responsibility. This approach is used successfully at St Anne's CEVC School where the headteacher plays an active role in ensuring that curriculum leaders take responsibility for advice in their subject. The following shows the way in which this responsibility is incorporated into job descriptions for curriculum leaders.

St Anne's CEVC School

CURRICULUM JOB LEADER DESCRIPTION: HUMANITIES (HISTORY, GEOGRAPHY, ENVIRONMENTAL EDUCATION, INTERNATIONAL EDUCATION)

Purpose
To further the aims of the school, underpinned by the value statement (Ethos) of the School Family working within the published policies.

General Responsibilities
1. Exhibit enthusiasm for Humanities and be an exemplary teacher in that subject in own class.

2. 2.1 Advise Head regarding philosophy, methodology, resources and assessment.
   2.2 Monitor work in Humanities and report annually to the Head for the Governors.

3. 3.1 Demonstrate ability to organise, guide and support staff in the operation of the school policy relating to Humanities.
   3.2 Support staff out of classroom or in classroom by working alongside them, or helping with a small group of pupils or leading the class if necessary.

4. Review and revise where necessary the school's scheme of work annually ensuring continuity and progression and appropriately differentiated activities for less able and more able children.

5. 5.1 Develop Humanities as an integral part of the curriculum and liaise with other curriculum leaders

   5.2 Liaise with Head and Deputy Head, and assist class teachers in planning for cross curricular topics.

6. Maintain and extend the resources in school.

7. Keep abreast of developments in Humanities and consider their relevance to this school in particular.

8 Liaise with cluster schools and other relevant bodies.

9 Make presentations to Governors and/or parents as required.

Review
This job description will be reviewed at appropriate intervals (normally one year).

In small schools such luxuries of choice are often unavailable and the SENCO looks after the most able as part of his or her role. SENCO responsibility also has some strengths. There is a certain logic in one person having responsibility for all children who need special care and attention. Many SENCOs are highly skilled at dealing with the individual needs of children, and the individual needs of able children are often best addressed using similar target-setting and review procedures. The major disadvantage, and it is a significant one, is the way in which able children usually come at the bottom of the list of the SENCO's concerns. The needs of other SEN children may be seen as more pressing, both because of their difficulty in accessing lessons and because of the legal demands of the special needs legislation as outlined in the *Code of Practice*. Able children, whilst they may not be being appropriately stretched, are at least compliant in class. This means their needs may be addressed less frequently and less systematically than the SEN categories listed in the *Code of Practice*.

If a decision is made to give the SENCO responsibility for able children, then the headteacher needs to ensure that the SENCO's load is manageable and that the needs of able children are given appropriate consideration and time. Of course SENCO responsibility has the same potential difficulties regarding ownership as any other coordinator role; other teachers feel less responsible. *A coordinator should coordinate work undertaken by the school, not take sole responsibility for that work.*

In an ideal world responsibility would follow the model shown in Figure 6.2. In reality compromises may need to be made. The headteacher and governors need to make those decisions in full recognition of the implications, and to discuss with staff their responsibilities in the chosen model. Figure 6.2 illustrates possible roles and responsibilities within primary schools.

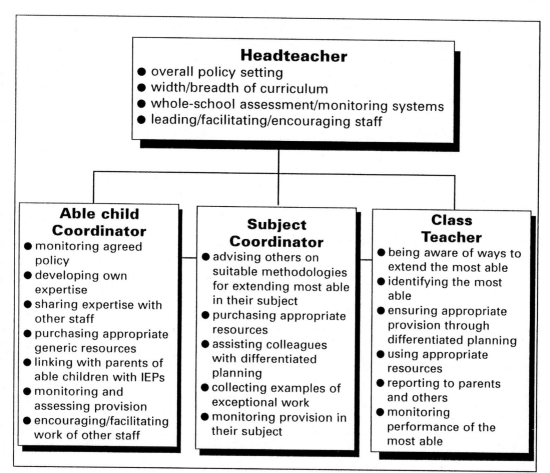

Figure 6.2 Roles and responsibilities in the primary school

Whole-school systems for managing and monitoring provision

Potter and Powell (1992) suggest that 95 per cent of what a school does is maintain existing systems and provision and 5 per cent may be described as development. If this analysis is correct then there is a strong case for making sure that systems established during a development phase are effective. They will be the basis for future maintenance and continuing provision. Traditionally, some primary schools have felt that as small units their need for systems is less acute than that of their secondary school colleagues. In some senses this may be so; certainly communication is generally easier in a smaller unit. However, good systems have some clear advantages. They save time because maintenance, review and development are built into the cycle and therefore occur regularly and naturally. They also help to gain clarity of purpose in that they are established to fulfil a particular function.

Systems which need to be considered in respect of able children are:

- staff development and deployment
- school documentation

- medium- and short-term planning
- monitoring of individuals
- identification of potential
- assessment
- purchase of resources
- finance
- monitoring and reporting.

Staff development and deployment

The single most important element in establishing good provision for able children is good teachers. They must be enthusiastic, organized, prepared to share ideas with others and have high expectations of the children in their care. Interviews with able adults, reflecting on their own education, provide clear evidence of the teacher either as a source of inspiration or a destructive force. Playwright Kay Mellor writing in the *Times Educational Supplement* (April, 1996) describes how at age 9, she had a story returned by a teacher with a comment describing it as 'very silly'. She did not write anything again for five years. Able children often produce work which is out of the ordinary and it can be dismissed as not fulfilling the anticipated criteria. A sensitive teacher might look beyond the obvious and spot potential.

It is interesting to note that some teachers seem to 'produce' able children. Perhaps it is because they are constantly looking for children to demonstrate signs of ability or perhaps they offer classroom opportunities which encourage children to excel. Either way, year by year they always have able children in their classrooms. These kinds of teachers are not restricted to a particular age group. They can be located anywhere in the school, from reception to Year 6. Interestingly, a good Year 6 teacher can unearth talent which has never been evident lower down the school. Equally, a good Year 2 teacher may recognize ability, but by Year 6 the school may consider that child to have 'plateaued out'. Perhaps this is the case, but it is also possible that the school is not providing challenge in Key Stage 2. Good teachers are 'talent spotters', constantly looking for signs of ability and setting high targets.

Recruiting teachers who are good teachers of the most able is important. A body of evidence is emerging to suggest that in order to be a good teacher of able children it is necessary to have very good teaching ability. Teachers need a solid base upon which to build extension skills. If they are not sure which concepts they are trying to convey then they will not be able to come up with additional concepts to challenge the most able. A question to candidates at interview either about able children or expectations can help to ensure that new staff have appropriate attitudes.

Dealing with existing staff can sometimes be a greater management problem, both in terms of where they are located within the school and opportunities for professional development. A whole-school policy on able children really does help individual teachers to play their part more effectively.

A major problem for teachers in the primary school concerns teaching such a wide curriculum (Eyre and Fuller, 1993). Most teachers are highly effective in some curriculum areas and sound in others. Whilst this is broadly as might be expected, it does have specific implications for able children. Children whose talents lie in the areas of the teacher's greatest effectiveness receive good quality extension opportunities. Children whose talents lie in the area of 'sound' provision will have less opportunity for extension work. In short, the able mathematician in the class of a teacher with a maths degree will usually be extended; able artists in the same class may not.

From the management perspective, two clear issues emerge. First, in the case of exceptionally able individuals, the child's progression route through the school may be linked to the expertise of particular teachers. Where a choice of teacher is available the decision should be influenced by the child's needs. Second, the more complex issue of developing staff expertise: staff need to be supported in their non-specialist areas and also given opportunities to develop greater skills in these areas. The role of both the subject coordinator and inservice training need some careful thought here. In primary schools the subject coordinators are often unable to support the teaching of their subjects, throughout the school, because of a shortage of non-contact time. They often advise on the purchase of resources, etc., but are not particularly effective in developing their colleagues' practice. They may not help with medium- or short-term planning for example. If good extension is to be made available in their subject throughout the school they will need to help their colleagues to plan.

Individual teachers need to be aware of their subject strengths and weaknesses and of the implications for able children. *All teachers should be encouraged to seek help from the subject coordinator in subjects where they do not feel confident. Any teacher who thinks he or she is good at all subjects should be viewed with extreme caution!*

Other issues for management consideration include the use of long courses to increase teacher subject knowledge in some curriculum areas; a lack of subject knowledge can mean that children are not introduced to the higher levels of the National Curriculum.

School documentation

In an integrated approach, the needs of able children should be reflected in all subject documentation in the same way as SEN. This facilitates the move towards inclusive provision and reminds the school community of the need to make provision. Reference should be made in the school aims and also in the prospectus. A typical prospectus comment might be along the lines of the that produced by St Anne's CEVC School, Bristol.

Able and Talented Children.

The school aims that every child works towards its potential and to that end activities and tasks are differentiated throughout the school.

Able children may have extension activities relating to core subjects or topic work as appropriate for their ability and teachers will generally discuss this with parents in advance. The school recognizes that some children have individual talents and these may be reinforced through school activities or through specific opportunities within the school day. A copy of the school policy relating to Able and Talented children is available in the school office.

Reference to extension opportunities should also be made in subject policies and those for cross-curricular themes. A reading policy, for example, should discuss not only how to support emergent readers but also how to extend independent readers. This process is crucial to ensuring that the needs of the most able are considered whenever a subject or issue is being addressed in school. Failure to incorporate this aspect into existing school documentation will lead to fragmented or 'bolt-on' provision, with all its inherent progression problems.

Medium- and short-term planning

The school's planning documentation needs a column or space for extension. At the medium-term level this will probably consist of elements of the topic or module which are to be covered in addition to, or in place of, part of the core. It might also include higher level concepts which most children are not expected to reach, perhaps in some cases accessing aspects of the next Key Stage.

Extension should also appear in the short-term planning, even if the planned extension is informal. This system encourages staff to remember to plan for extension and allows the headteacher to monitor extension opportunities easily. If the planning sheets have an extension box or column, then teachers will use it.

Monitoring of individuals (individual education plans)

Some able children need their progress tracked very carefully and systematically. This can be for a number of reasons:

- they may be exceptionally able and therefore need special targets to be set,
- they may be very able but have particular deficits, e.g. poor writing or organizational skills,
- they may be intellectually able but have social or emotional problems,
- they may lack confidence or self-esteem.

In order for a school to achieve this effectively, some suitable form of record keeping is needed. Unlike SEN, there is no legal requirement to create individual education plans for able children, but it makes the work of the teacher and the coordinator much easier. It also facilitates good transfer between classes and schools. It is particularly important if the child is accessing the next stage of the National Curriculum, as this affects teacher planning. A typical form for tracking the exceptionally able is given in Figure 6.3. Targets are generally a mix of intellectual and social and/or organizational, and are reviewed termly. Some children may only be on the forms for a limited time until a problem is resolved; others, especially the exceptionally able, will always need the form to ensure appropriate progress is being made.

Assessment

School assessment systems should recognize high levels of achievement as well as expected levels. The senior management needs to ensure that all assessment used in school has the facility to show outstanding achievement. This includes reading or spelling assessments which sometimes have a ceiling, e.g. the reading age does not go beyond age 12. If these kinds of tests are used by the school then additional assessments may be needed for those children who score a maximum. Assessments which simply show whether a child can or cannot complete a task sometimes do not allow a child to demonstrate a more thorough understanding.

Example:

A test which a 4-year-old was given to assess her knowledge of colours asked the child to choose another brick to add to the row consisting of a red, a blue and a green brick. She took a long time before deciding to add a yellow brick and correctly named the colour yellow. The tester, curious as to why she took so long, asked about her choice of yellow. 'Well', she explained, 'I was looking for a six letter colour because red has three, blue four and green five.'

This is typical of the problems with some assessments. The opportunity to demonstrate knowledge beyond the expected is simply not available.

One confusion regarding assessments is between those that measure ability and those that measure achievement. Some tests, for example, NFER non-verbal tests, test ability; others, such as SATs, test performance. The school's assessment procedures should include some assessment of performance and also some of ability. Staff need to recognize which is being assessed if underachievement is to be spotted.

A useful assessment activity is for the school to keep a portfolio of outstanding work. This helps staff to develop their assessment skills and to recognize the difference between, say, a well executed piece of work (neat and tidy) and a piece which shows originality or draws upon knowledge previously learnt.

Resources

Appropriate resources are an important feature of good provision. Systems need to be in place for the regular purchase both of generic material and equipment which encourage thinking, and of subject-specific resources. Resources are not an answer to provision in themselves but are needed if busy teachers are to create extension tasks.

Finance

In the financial planning for the school, consideration needs to be given to provision for the most able. Good provision does have financial implications: purchase of books and equipment, staff training, and possibly withdrawal groups. Governors and headteachers may wish to consider a 'budget line' for the most able.

Monitoring and reporting

These systems too should take account of the most able. School monitoring of subjects or themes should include monitoring of the most able. Moderation of work should include some examples from the most able. Monitoring of opportunities should include opportunities for the most able. Monitoring of resources should include resources for the most able and monitoring of teaching should include the teaching of the most able. In short, provision for the most able should be integral to all school systems. This ensures that a school's aim to provide appropriately for all its children is a reality.

Reporting on the achievements of children is an important aspect of good provision. Recognizing and rewarding a wide variety of achievements leads to raised self-esteem and

OXFORDSHIRE COUNTY COUNCIL
Education Service
LEARNING COUNTYWIDE

Exceptionally Able Progress Sheet

Pupil Name ______ **D.O.B.** / /

School ______ **Pupil Age at Referral** ______

Evidence

OQSA
OXFORDSHIRE QUALITY SCHOOLS ASSOCIATION

Figure 6.3 Monitoring form

Termly Targets

Term

Review

Signed

Figure 6.3 Continued

greater motivation. A school system of rewards should recognize and reward not only academic achievement but also leadership, hard work, interpersonal skills and organizational skills. The wider the range of areas recognized the greater the number of children who can achieve. The principles of the reward system have to be agreed by all staff if it is to be effective. Gold stars cease to have the desired motivating effect if they degenerate into a bribe to keep children under control.

Whole-school opportunities which enrich and extend

The main part of a child's experience in the primary school may be with his or her class teacher, but what is on offer outside of the ordinary class is also a significant aspect of a child's schooling. Many able children, when interviewed, indicate that they really enjoy these additional opportunities because they allow for more independence and the development of new skills. So, when a school is thinking about its provision for able children, these opportunities should be taken into account. This is an area of real strength for many schools, which should be celebrated.

- Regular activities at whole-school level
- School-wide initiatives
- Visitors to school
- Educational trips
- Clubs and societies
- Competitions.

Regular activities at whole-school level

Most schools have a regular calendar of activities including school plays, sports days, assemblies, etc. Class assemblies provide an opportunity for those who excel at reading or acting and can provide a chance for a small group to do some independent planning. Both these and school plays can be a real opportunity for those with leadership or organizational skills. If your school is looking to recognize and develop a wide range of abilities, here is a useful arena.

Sports day is for some children the one chance in the year to excel in front of others. Children with physical ability are not always good academically. A chance to shine on the sports field may help to improve confidence in other areas. Academically able children are sometimes physically uncoordinated and sports day can be hard. A good school supports children who find sport difficult just as they do children who find academic work difficult.

School-wide initiatives

These are often tremendously motivating for children and can lead to outstanding work in a variety of contexts. The chance to design new equipment for the playground, to design and build a wildlife garden, to reorganize the school library – these and many other ideas lead to the use of discussion, high level decision making and evaluative skills. The more children are involved in the life and community of the school the more they respect and enjoy it.

One headteacher of my acquaintance regularly asks his Key Stage 2 pupils to draft letters home to parents on such issues as school trips, etc. They have to decide on the information to be conveyed, the language to be used and any reply needed. Another head of a small school allows Key Stage 2 children to answer the telephone. They take messages and deal with visitors as part of their leadership experience.

Visitors to school

Many schools have a variety of visitors, from authors in Book Week to the local community policeman. Using experts allows children to explore ideas in depth. Experts, because they know their subject so well, are often able to convey complex ideas with great clarity. They are seldom floored by a question and convey their subject with great enthusiasm.

These are often very significant events for able children. They may be the start of a lifelong interest in a particular subject or may simply provide an idea which lies dormant in a child's mind for years before re-emerging at a later date. To quote one teacher:

In a Year 5 class I commented on a poem a child was writing. She informed me that she was a poet. I asked if she had always liked poetry and she replied that she had only been a poet since the previous year. Pursuing this further, I discovered that her interest had been sparked by the visit to school of a local poet. She had been captivated by his work and had been writing poetry ever since. As she put it, 'I listened to his poems and I thought, "I could do that". So I started writing and I've been writing ever since.'

Educational trips

These have a similar power for bringing learning to life. They also provide a chance to develop interpersonal skills. Offering a broad range of experience is so important. You will never know that you have a particular aptitude or skill unless you have been given the opportunity to try. Perhaps one reason that private schools with small classes are so successful is because they can offer enough activities for most children to find a strength.

Clubs and societies

Many schools provide a wide range of clubs and societies where children can either learn new subjects and skills or develop existing ones. Traditionally, school clubs have been primarily for sport and music. These clubs allow children with talent in those particular areas to reach a level of expertise which it would be difficult to foster in the ordinary classroom context. In music this is often as part of a recorder group or school orchestra which allows those with a musical talent to play together. Such groups greatly enhance the life of the school as well as helping musical children fulfil their potential. Sport too builds team skills and interpersonal ability in addition to sporting skills, and playing for the school can allow children a level of responsibility which they do not experience elsewhere.

Other types of clubs may be less common in schools but where they are found they are very successful. Those with abilities in the traditionally academic areas may not have many opportunities through after-school clubs. Where schools have created maths clubs, chess clubs, French clubs or even philosophy clubs, there are some children who really benefit from these. Frideswide Middle School in Oxford has a Latin Club which is a very popular option for some children and has led to some ex-Frideswide students taking Latin GCSE at a later stage in their schooling.

Significant expertise can also be developed in the arts. It is sometimes possible to encourage local artists to work with children in after-school clubs. In one school a group of Key Stage 1 children were working with a local artist on water colour painting and were able to discuss their pictures using the appropriate technical language and making use of a range of technical skills which would be unfamiliar to most adults.

Perhaps the greatest strength of school clubs lies in the opportunity they provide for children of a variety of ages to work together in a relaxed setting. Because such clubs are voluntary, children are there from choice and are keen to work hard and make maximum progress, a situation which is a joy for teacher and child alike. In considering the range of clubs it is useful to look both at those which will be offered consistently and those which may be only a short taster course. Some things lend themselves well to a six-week or one-term block, and finding willing teachers for short blocks is much easier than for indefinite periods.

Competitions

These provide an opportunity for those with talent to excel. Competitions can be used in a variety of ways. There are whole-school competitions that occur at certain times of the year or linked to another project, e.g. painting eggs at Easter or writing a poem in Book Week. There are class- or year-based competitions linked to class projects or activities, e.g. technology competitions or those linked to an historical project. There are competitions offered externally like the Royal Mail Letter Writing Competition which a whole class or school may try for and there are competitions advertised in the *Times Educational Supplement* and other parts of the educational press.

In reviewing the competitions on offer in school, two areas are worth considering. First a look at the balance. It may be possible, without too much extra work, to offer other types of competitions, maths for example. The maths coordinator could offer a problem for each section of the school. This is not arduous since many such problems can easily be found in maths activity books. Answers can be displayed and children encouraged to discuss the solutions. This is a useful way of encouraging mathematical thinking generally as well as providing real challenge for the mathematically able.

Second schools can use competitions to encourage individuals. Rather than making a decision on whether the school will or will not enter a competition, a headteacher or subject coordinator may look at whether it would be suitable for particular individuals within the school.

A useful staff meeting activity is to encourage all staff to list the opportunities offered at whole-school or extra-curricular level, over the last year.

Withdrawal activities

An initial response when starting to look seriously at provision for able children, is to consider the possibility of creating withdrawal opportunities. This is the way that most primary schools have traditionally dealt with addressing the needs of particular groups of pupils and seems a sensible way forward for able children.

From the management perspective the major difficulty with this approach is linked to cost. Withdrawal groups are always a costly aspect of school provision, unless they are run by voluntary help. If withdrawal opportunities are to be useful in terms of provision for the most able then they need to be carefully planned, intellectually challenging and consistent. These elements are difficult to achieve with voluntary help and therefore withdrawal groups for able pupils tend to need professional staffing. Occasionally a school may be lucky enough to have a volunteer who can lead an able child group, but such help is rare.

A reasonable philosophical approach might suggest that if able children need some opportunities to work at a rapid pace with others of like ability, and this is not readily available in the classroom, then it should be provided elsewhere. Able pupils have as much right as other pupils to an appropriate education. Evidence would suggest, however, that even when a school has created such opportunities, they are axed as soon as any budget cuts occur.

Oxfordshire LEA in its 1995 *Survey of Provision for Able Pupils in 12 Oxford City Schools* notes, 'Funding cuts have taken their toll. In the worst cases this has caused the scrapping of enrichment programmes' (Shields, 1995, p.10). This is because many schools see withdrawal groups for able children as desirable but not essential – at the luxury end of the market. For the headteacher the question is whether, without withdrawal groups, effective provision can be made. If effective provision necessitates withdrawal groups then they are not expendable and should not be seen as an easy option in making budget reductions.

Ideally it should be possible for all needs to be met within the context of the ordinary classroom but a variety of factors may make that impossible:

- class size,
- organizational composition, e.g. vertical age groups,
- pupil composition, e.g. bottom-heavy classes,
- staff subject expertise,
- resources.

Therefore, in considering withdrawal groups the initial question must be, 'Can we manage without them?' A negative answer to this would make them an integral feature of provision and therefore a permanent fixture in the school. A positive answer may make them unnecessary. The most likely answer would be between these two points. Reasonable provision could be made in the classroom but it would be greatly enhanced by withdrawal opportunities. If this is the situation then withdrawal opportunities need to be planned to bring maximum benefit at the least cost.

Who to withdraw and for what?

Whenever withdrawal opportunities are created thought needs to be given to sustainability. Some opportunities are for an agreed period of time; others are set in response to particular circumstances and may have long-term implications. Withdrawal opportunities are usually created for one of the following reasons:

- in response to an individual or small group of very able children in a class,
- to maximize staff or other adult expertise,

- to develop specific abilities across the age groups,
- as part of whole-school planned provision.

In the first instance this may arise because a single child or a group of children is present in a class and is operating at a level and speed which are considerably in excess of the rest of the class. This often happens with a group of very able mathematicians. The gap between the top and bottom of the class is so great that some additional support is needed. This means that the able mathematicians may have small-group work once or twice a week and the least able twice or three times. In a large school such a group may be created from a range of classes; mixing two age groups of able pupils is not usually a problem, especially if the younger group are very able. This type of provision has long-term implications. Will the group continue to exist as they move through the school? Will they always need this type of provision? Are there particular age groups where this kind of problem is most acute? Is it reasonable for one group to have all the withdrawal opportunities? These are the types of questions to consider before embarking on this type of withdrawal.

Where staff or adult expertise is the reason for creating the opportunities, other issues may need consideration. Children will be selected for the group based on their ability in that particular area and offered a unique chance to take the subject into greater depth. This is especially valuable in Years 5 and 6 where the subject knowledge of the teacher may restrict performance. Able scientists working with a science specialist may achieve more highly than in a general classroom situation. Subject-specialist opportunities are invariably enhancing. Their availability may be limited by finance or by opportunity; the school's expert in technology may move to another school and be replaced by a colleague with different skills.

Where withdrawal is used to develop particular skills across the age groups, one child's needs or those of a small group often act as a catalyst. A very mature infant may need opportunities for discussion with older children. An exceptional reader may benefit from chances to discuss books with other such readers. Creating such a group often starts with the child for whom provision is needed, but other children selected for the group will undoubtedly benefit. Age ceases to be an issue here; children are linked by common interest and enthusiasm.

The final reason for the creation of withdrawal groups is as part of a planned school approach. If able children need opportunities to work with others of like ability, then this may be the best, or in some cases only, way to provide this opportunity. This type of opportunity can be highly effective but it does need careful planning.

Making the most of withdrawal opportunities

In order to ensure that withdrawal opportunities are used effectively the headteacher needs to be alert to certain key issues.

Purpose

Are staff clear about why such provision is needed and what they are hoping to achieve? Sometimes withdrawal is seen as a way to deal with a difficult problem. The able mathematicians need more extension; if we give them a withdrawal session once a week this should solve the problem. This is part of an off-loading process with little thought being given to either the content of the sessions or the link with class maths teaching.

Content

Ideally withdrawal sessions should either allow children to work in more depth, or cover areas not being covered by the rest of the class, or learn new skills. The second of these is the usual context for a withdrawal group, although the other two may in fact be more valuable. If, for example, sessions are used to learn new skills, e.g. critical analysis of text, then these skills can be applied in subsequent lessons rather than the withdrawal being an end in itself.

Planning and evaluation

These sessions should have clear learning objectives and show progression in the same way as other work. They should not be a bolt-on approach to the curriculum as this has proved ineffective. It should be possible for the headteacher to see the link between withdrawal activities and the classwork of these children. Sometimes withdrawal has offered a chance to explore a subject in a way which is exciting but which cannot be linked to class activity. The result of this can be greater frustration in class. A child commented to me: 'I love the maths extension sessions but I hate ordinary maths – it is boring'. Something is wrong here: either the class sessions or the extensions are inappropriate. Certainly there is no link or continuity between them and the child is not obtaining good provision.

The advantages and disadvantages of withdrawal groups can be contrasted as follows:

Advantages	*Disadvantages*
able to work with others of like ability	financial and staffing costs
pace is likely to be rapid	effect on other children
chance to work with an adult	possible bolt-on nature
opportunity to explore ideas in depth	continuity problems
chance to learn advanced skills/techniques	raised expectations of group
intellectual excitement	
high expectation	

For withdrawal groups to work well they should be available at various times to a variety of children. They should be an area for which the class teacher takes overall responsibility in terms of both content and monitoring. They should be a response to improving classroom extension either for a subject or a group of children, rather than the only way of providing extension.

Summary

For a school to be truly effective in its provision for able children it will need to consider provision for the most able as a feature of every aspect of the school. Each time a school subject is discussed or a policy created the school should consider its implications for the most able. Staff should be able to articulate readily the school's approach to able pupils in all subject areas as well as in generic areas and have a clear sense of individual children's abilities or talents. Information on the school's approach should be shared with parents and governors and with the children. High expectation of children's achievements should be a major feature of the school.

Here is a checklist for headteachers and senior managers, taken from Eyre (1997):

- All staff have an awareness of the key issues in the education of able children
- Staff and governors have received training on the education of able children
- The school has someone with coordinating responsibility for able children
- Systems exist for the tracking of individual exceptionally able children
- Able children are mentioned in the prospectus
- Able children are mentioned in subject policies
- A school policy for able children exists
- Staff development and deployment show an awareness of able child issues
- An element of the budget recognizes the needs of able children
- Extension exists in medium- and short-term planning
- Systems exist to facilitate the identification of ability
- Work from able children is discussed at staff meetings from time to time
- A portfolio of outstanding work exists
- Whole-school opportunities are reviewed to ensure breadth and balance
- Achievement is recognized and rewarded.

Appendix 1

Writing a Policy for the More Able

The policy should include both the school's philosophical approach and the practical mechanisms that convert policy into practice.

1. General rationale
- why such a policy is needed
- where it links into general school aims and philosophy.

2. Aims
What the school aims to provide for able pupils, e.g.:
- entitlement to appropriate education
- work at higher cognitive levels
- opportunities to develop specific skills or talents
- a concern for the whole child – social and intellectual.

3. Definitions

4. General overall approach
e.g. in-class provision, setting, withdrawal.

5. Identification and monitoring schemes

6. Organizational responses
- acceleration
- working with older pupils
- withdrawal across year groups
- provision for exceptional pupils, e.g. mentoring.

7. In-class approach
- enrichment/extension
- working with others of like ability
- differentiation
- challenge within subject areas
- differentiated homework.

8. Out-of-class activities
- enrichment days or residentials
- school clubs
- musical and sporting opportunities.

9. Personal and social education

10. Responsibility for coordinating and monitoring progress
e.g. named coordinator or class teacher.

11. Process for review and development

12. Use of outside agencies for training, provision, etc.

Appendix 2

Marston Middle School, Oxford: Policy for Able Pupils

1. Statement of philosophy
Our school aims state that we endeavour

- to help our pupils develop their personalities, skills and abilities intellectually and socially,
- to provide teaching which makes learning challenging and enjoyable and enables pupils to realise their potential,

and that

- we are committed to working for quality and equality of opportunity.

In the light of these aims it should be clear that we are committed to providing an environment which encourages **all** pupils to maximise their potential and this clearly includes pupils who display some form of giftedness.

2. Definition
A gifted pupil is one who demonstrates a significantly higher level of ability than most pupils of the same age in one or more curriculum areas or in any of the following:

- physical talent
- artistic talent
- mechanical ingenuity
- leadership
- high intelligence
- creativity

(Eric Ogilvie, 1973)

It is worth remembering that gifted pupils can be:

- good all-rounders
- high achievers in one area
- of high ability but with low motivation
- of good verbal ability but poor writing skills
- very able with short attention span
- very able with poor social skills
- keen to disguise their abilities

(Deborah Eyre, 1993)

3. Identification

A gifted pupil is identified through teacher assessment and judgement. This professional assessment is carried out through:

- analysis of information from first schools
- discussion of pupils with colleagues
- discussion with the child
- consultation with parents/guardians
- ongoing assessment using open/differentiated tasks
- careful record keeping
- collation of evidence (i.e. individual pupils' work)
- use of the Marked Aptitudes Grid….

Testing of individual pupils is carried out where appropriate.

4. Strategies

4.1 Institutional level

Opportunities for extension and enrichment are built into all our schemes of work. We aim to:

- create an ethos where 'it is OK to be bright'
- encourage all pupils to become 'independent learners'. For able pupils in particular, the library provides an invaluable resource for private study and research
- be aware of the effects of ethnicity, bilingualism, gender and social circumstances on learning and high achievement
- use a variety of whole school strategies including:
  - enrichment weeks/special activities (when the normal timetable is suspended and cross-curricular projects are pursued which offer pupils more choice and responsibility)
  - occasionally allowing pupils to work with a different year group
  - withdrawal across year groups
  - provision for the exceptionally able, e.g. mentoring
  - giving pupils opportunities to serve on various working parties (e.g. Newsletter, Bully Court, Environment, Behaviour, etc.)
  - recognising achievement (teacher praise, Records of Achievement, Head's Commendation, etc.)

4.2 In the classroom

We understand the importance of establishing what prior knowledge, understanding and skills pupils have so as to avoid unnecessary repetition of work which is extremely demotivating.

We are aware that, especially in the older age group, there is peer pressure to under-achieve. We endeavour to combat this attitude whilst being sensitive to the need of many pupils to conform.

We are alert for the 'bright but lazy' pupil who could achieve excellent results if motivated and challenged. For **all** pupils, lack of motivation and challenge leads to boredom and often to behaviour problems.

Finally, we are aware of the danger of assuming that gifted pupils are easier to teach than other pupils.

The following strategies are employed where appropriate:

- varied and flexible pupil groupings, sometimes allowing able pupils to work together, sometimes allowing them to take particular roles in mixed-ability groups
- differentiation by task (including differentiated homework)
- differentiation by outcome
- setting individual targets

and most importantly:

- encouraging all pupils to become 'independent learners':
  - organising their own work
  - carrying out unaided tasks which stretch their capabilities
  - making choices about their work
  - developing the ability to evaluate their work and so become self critical.

Pupils' abilities should be recognized and valued. Appreciation of their achievements makes an important contribution to their development.

4.3 Out of the classroom

We aim to provide:

- a wide range of extra-curricular activities and clubs
- enrichment weeks and local and residential trips
- where possible, the use of outside agencies for training and provision.

5. Monitoring the effectiveness of this policy

This policy and its effectiveness will be reviewed regularly by a Staff Working Party.

Form tutors are responsible for maintaining documentation of pupils' progress and achievements. The Special Needs coordinator checks a random sample of pupils' files at least twice a year to ensure that appropriate records are being kept.

The Marked Aptitudes Grid

Staff are asked to use the Marked Aptitudes Grid in November and May each year. Collated results should form the basis for discussion by Key Stage teams.

For Key Stage 2 pupils the grid will consist of the six areas of giftedness listed in section 2 of the policy. For Key Stage 3 pupils the grid will also include assessments in each curriculum subject.

Staff should simply put a tick if in their opinion the pupil displays giftedness in that subject.

Bibliography

Adams, J., Eyre, D., Howell, J. and Raffan, J. (1987) *The Village of Eddington*, Wisbech: LDA Publications.

Alexander, R., Rose, J. and Woodhead, C. (1992) *Curriculum Organization and Classroom Practice in Primary Schools: A discussion paper*, London: DES.

Bennett, N. and Dunne, E. (1992) *Managing Classroom Groups*, Cheltenham: Stanley Thornes.

Bennett, N., Desforges, A., Cockburn, A. and Wilkinson, B. (1984) *The Quality of Pupils' Learning Experiences*, Hove: Lawrence Erlbaum Associates.

Blagg, N., Ballinger, M. and Gardner, R. (1988) *The Somerset Thinking Skills Course*, Oxford: Blackwell.

Bloom, B. (ed.) (1956) *Taxonomy of Educational Objectives*, Vol. 1, Harlow: Longman.

Bloom, B. (1985) *Developing Talent in Young People*, New York: Ballantine.

Bouchard, T. *et al.* (1990) 'Sources of human psychological differences', *Science*, **250**, 223–8.

Burgess, T. (1996) 'Are the Key Stage 1 mathematics SATs effective in identifying children of high mathematical ability?', B.Phil.Ed dissertation, University of Warwick.

Buzan, T. (1995) *Use Your Head*, London: BBC Publications.

Chambers, A. (1985) *Booktalk*, London: Bodley Head.

Chambers, A. (1993) *Tell Me*, Stroud: Thimble Press.

Creemers, B. P. M. (1994) *The Effective Classroom*, London: Cassell.

Crocker, A. C. (1988) 'The ability of young children to rank themselves for academic ability', *Educational Studies*, 14, 105–10.

Cropley, A. J. (1995) 'Actualizing creative intelligence', in Freeman, J. (ed.) *Actualizing Talent*, London: Cassell.

Dearing, R. (1996) *Review of 16–19 Qualifications*, London: HMSO.

Denton, C. and Postlethwaite, K. (1985) *Able Children – Identifying them in the classroom*, Windsor: NFER/Nelson.

DfEE (1994) *The Code of Practice on the Identification and Assessment of Special Educational Needs*, London: HMSO.

DfEE (1995) *The National Curriculum for England and Wales*, London: HMSO.

Evans, L. (1995) *Degrees of Disadvantage*, Oxford: NACE (National Association for Able Children in Education).

Eyre, D. (1994) *More Able Pupils in SEN Policy Statements*, Oxford: Oxspec (Oxfordshire LEA/Oxford Brookes University).

Eyre, D. (1995) *School Governors and More Able Children*, London: HMSO.

Eyre, D. (1997) 'Teaching able pupils', *Support for Learning*, forthcoming.

Eyre, D. and Fuller, M. (1993) *Year 6 Teachers and More Able Pupils*, Oxford: National Primary Centre.

Eyre, D. and Marjoram, T. (1990) *Enriching and Extending the National Curriculum.* London: Kogan Page.

Eysenck, H. J. (1981) *The Intelligence Controversy*, New York: John Wiley.

Feuerstein, R. (1980) *Instrumental Enrichment*, Baltimore, MD: University Park Press.

Fisher, R. (1987) *Problem Solving in Primary Schools*, Oxford: Blackwell.

Fisher, R. (1990) *Teaching Children to Think*, Cheltenham: Stanley Thornes.

Freeman, J. (1980) *Gifted Children*, London: Cassell.

Freeman, J. (1991) *Gifted Children Growing Up*, London: Cassell.

Freeman, J. (1995) 'Review of current thinking on the development of talent', in Freeman, J. (ed.) *Actualizing Talent*, London: Cassell.

Gagné, F. (1994) 'Gifts and talents: the value of peer nominations', keynote address, 4th International Conference of European Council for High Ability (ECHA), October, University of Nijmegen, The Netherlands.

Gallagher, J. J. (1985) *Teaching the Gifted Child*, Newton: Allyn and Bacon.

Gardner, H. (1983) *Frames of Mind*, London: Fontana Press.

Griffin, N. S., Curtiss, J., McKenzie, J., Maxfield, L. and Crawford M. (1995) 'Authentic assessment of able children using a regular classroom observation protocol', *Flying High*, 2, 34–42.

Guilford, J. P. (1950) 'Creativity', *American Psychologist*, 5, 444–54.

Guilford, J. P. (1967) *The Nature of Human Intelligence*, New York: McGraw Hill.

HMI (1978) *Primary Education in England: A survey of HM Inspectors of Schools*, London: HMSO.

HMI (1992) *Education Observed: The education of very able children in maintained schools*, London: HMSO.

Howe, M. (1995) 'What can we learn from the lives of geniuses?', in Freeman, J. (ed.) *Actualizing Talent*, London: Cassell.

Jensen, A. (1980) *Bias in Mental Testing*, New York: Free Press.

Kennard, R. (1996) *Teaching Mathematically Able Children*, Oxford: NACE (National Association for Able Children in Education).

Kent LEA (1996) *Able Children Handbook*, Tonbridge: Kent LEA.

Kerry, T. (1984) 'Primary and secondary tasks', *Gifted Education International*, 2, 116–18.

Krechevsky, M. and Gardner, H. (1990) 'The emergence and nurture of multiple intelligence', in Howe, M. (ed.) *Encouraging the Development of Exceptional Abilities and Talent*, Leicester: British Psychological Society.

Leyden, S. (1985) *Helping the Child of Exceptional Ability*, London: Routledge.

Lipman, M., Sharp, A. M. and Oscannyon, F. S. (1980) *Philosophy in the Classroom*, Philadelphia: Temple University Press.

Lunzer, E., Gardner, K., Davies, F. and Greene, T. (1984) *Learning from the Written Word*, London: Oliver and Boyd.

Monks, F. J. (1992) 'Development of gifted children: the issue of identification and programming', in Mönks, F. J. and Peters, W. (eds) *Talent for the Future*, Assen/Maastricht: Van Gorcum.

Montgomery, D. (1996) *Educating the Able*, London: Cassell

Murris, K. (1992) *Philosophy with Picture Books*, London: Infonet Publications.

NACE/DfEE Project (1996) *Supporting the Education of Able Pupils in Maintained Schools*, Oxford: NACE (National Association for Able Children in Education).

National Commission on Education (1996) *Success Against the Odds*, London: Routledge.

National Primary Centre (1995) *Baseline Assessment*, Oxford: National Primary Centre.

Nebesnuick, S. (1993) 'The secondary transfer of able pupils', M.Ed. dissertation, Oxford Brookes University.

O'Connell, H. (1996) *Supporting More Able Pupils*, Scunthorpe: Desk Top Publishing.

OFSTED (1994) *Improving Schools*, London: HMSO.

Oxfordshire LEA (1988) *Oxfordshire Achievement Project*, Oxford: Oxfordshire LEA.

Paul Hamlyn Foundation (1993) *Learning to Succeed*, Oxford: Heinemann.

Potter, D. and Powell, G. (1992) *Managing a Better School*, Oxford: Heinemann.

Renzulli, J. S. (1977) *The Triad Enrichment Model. A guide for developing defensible programs for the gifted and talented*, Mansfield Center, CN: Creative Learning Press.

Royal Meteorological Society (1996) *Weather Log, January 1996*, Reading: Royal Meteorological Society.

Rudduck, J. (1995) 'What can pupils tell us about school improvement?', Lecture at the London Institute Conference, London.

Sammons, P., Hillman, J. and Mortimore, P. (1996) *Key Characteristics of Effective Schools*, Ringwood: B and MBC Distribution Services.

Shayer, M. and Adey, P. (1981) *Towards a Science of Science Teaching*, Oxford: Heinemann.

Shields, C. (1995) *A Survey of Provision for More Able Pupils in 12 Oxford City Schools*, Oxford: Oxspec (Oxfordshire LEA/ Oxford Brookes University).

Sternberg, R. (1982) *Handbook of Human Intelligence*, Cambridge: Cambridge University Press.

Sternberg, R. (1985) *Beyond IQ. A triarchic theory of human intelligence*, Cambridge: Cambridge University Press.

Teare, B. (1996) *Writing a School Policy*, Oxford: NACE (National Association for Able Children in Education).

Terman, L. M. (1925) *Genetic Studies of Genius. Volume 1: Mental and physical traits of a thousand gifted children*, Stanford, CA: Stanford University Press.

Thorndike, R. L. and Hagen, E. (1978) *Cognitive Ability Test*, Windsor: NFER/Nelson.

Tilsley, P. (1995) 'The use of tests and test data in the identification or recognition of high ability', *Flying High*, 2, 43–50.

Torrance, E. P. (1965) *Gifted Children in the Classroom*, New York: Collier.

Urban, K. (1990) 'Recent trends in creativity research', *European Journal of High Ability*, 1, 99–113.

Vygotsky, L. S. (1978) *Mind in Society*, Cambridge, MA: Harvard University Press.

Wragg, E. C. and Brown, G. (1993) *Questioning*, London: Routledge.

Index

Printed in the United Kingdom
by Lightning Source UK Ltd.
120088UK00008B/135